Full Color on Every Page!

Computers Simplified™ 4th Edition

IDG's 3-D Visual™ Series

IDG BOOKS From **maranGraphics™**

IDG Books Worldwide, Inc.
An International Data Group Company
Foster City, CA • Indianapolis • Chicago • Southlake, TX

Computers Simplified™, 4th Edition

Published by
IDG Books Worldwide, Inc.
An International Data Group Company
919 E. Hillsdale Blvd., Suite 400
Foster City, CA 94404
(650) 655-3000

Library of Congress Catalog Card No.: 98-072283

ISBN: 0-7645-6042-5

Printed in the United States of America

10 9 8 7 6 5 4

Distributed in the United States by IDG Books Worldwide, Inc.

Distributed by Transworld Publishers Limited in the United Kingdom; by IDG Norge Books for Norway; by IDG Sweden Books for Sweden; by Woodslane Pty. Ltd. for Australia; by Woodslane (NZ) Ltd. for New Zealand; by Addison Wesley Longman Singapore Pte Ltd. for Singapore, Malaysia, Thailand, Indonesia and Korea; by Norma Comunicaciones S.A. for Colombia; by Intersoft for South Africa; by International Thomson Publishing for Germany, Austria and Switzerland; by Toppan Company Ltd. for Japan; by Distribuidora Cuspide for Argentina; by Livraria Cultura for Brazil; by Ediciencia S.A. for Ecuador; by Ediciones ZETA S.C.R. Ltda. for Peru; by WS Computer Publishing Corporation, Inc., for the Philippines; by Unalis Corporation for Taiwan; by Contemporanea de Ediciones for Venezuela; by Computer Book & Magazine Store for Puerto Rico; by Express Computer Distributors for the Caribbean and West Indies. Authorized Sales Agent: Anthony Rudkin Associates for the Middle East and North Africa.

For corporate orders, please call maranGraphics at 800-469-6616.

For general information on IDG Books Worldwide's books in the U.S., please call our Consumer Customer Service department at 800-762-2974.

For reseller information, including discounts and premium sales, please call our Reseller Customer Service department at 800-434-3422.

For information on where to purchase IDG Books Worldwide's books outside the U.S., please contact our International Sales department at 650-655-3200 or fax 650-655-3297.

For information on foreign language translations, please contact our Foreign & Subsidiary Rights department at 650-655-3021 or fax 650-655-3281.

For sales inquiries and special prices for bulk quantities, please contact our Sales department at 650-655-3200.

For information on using IDG Books Worldwide's books in the classroom or for ordering examination copies, please contact our Educational Sales department at 800-434-2086 or fax 317-596-5499.

For press review copies, author interviews, or other publicity information, please contact our Public Relations department at 650-655-3000 or fax 650-655-3299.

For authorization to photocopy items for corporate, personal, or educational use, please contact maranGraphics at 800-469-6616.

Trademark Acknowledgments

©1998
maranGraphics, Inc.

The 3-D illustrations are the copyright of maranGraphics, Inc.

U.S. Corporate Sales	**U.S. Trade Sales**
Contact maranGraphics at (800) 469-6616 or Fax (905) 890-9434.	Contact IDG Books at (800) 434-3422 or (415) 655-3000.

Welcome to the world of IDG Books Worldwide.

IDG Books Worldwide, Inc., is a subsidiary of International Data Group, the world's largest publisher of computer-related information and the leading global provider of information services on information technology. IDG was founded more than 25 years ago and now employs more than 8,500 people worldwide. IDG publishes more than 270 computer publications in over 75 countries (see listing below). More than 90 million people read one or more IDG publications each month.

Launched in 1990, IDG Books Worldwide is today the #1 publisher of best-selling computer books in the United States. We are proud to have received eight awards from the Computer Press Association in recognition of editorial excellence and three from Computer Currents' First Annual Readers' Choice Awards. Our best-selling ...For Dummies® series has more than 25 million copies in print with translations in 30 languages. IDG Books Worldwide, through a joint venture with IDG's Hi-Tech Beijing, became the first U.S. publisher to publish a computer book in the People's Republic of China. In record time, IDG Books Worldwide has become the first choice for millions of readers around the world who want to learn how to better manage their businesses.

Our mission is simple: Every one of our books is designed to bring extra value and skill-building instructions to the reader. Our books are written by experts who understand and care about our readers. The knowledge base of our editorial staff comes from years of experience in publishing, education, and journalism - experience which we use to produce books for the '90s. In short, we care about books, so we attract the best people. We devote special attention to details such as audience, interior design, use of icons, and illustrations. And because we use an efficient process of authoring, editing, and desktop publishing our books electronically, we can spend more time ensuring superior content and spend less time on the technicalities of making books.

You can count on our commitment to deliver high-quality books at competitive prices on topics you want to read about. At IDG Books Worldwide, we continue in the IDG tradition of delivering quality for more than 25 years. You'll find no better book on a subject than one from IDG Books Worldwide.

John Kilcullen
President and CEO
IDG Books Worldwide, Inc.

IDG Books Worldwide, Inc., is a subsidiary of International Data Group, the world's largest publisher of computer-related information and the leading global provider of information services on information technology. International Data Group publishes over 276 computer publications in over 75 countries. Ninety million people read one or more International Data Group publications each month. International Data Group's publications include: Argentina: Annuario de Informatica, Computerworld Argentina, PC World Argentina; Australia: Australian Macworld, Client/Server Journal, Computer Living, Computerworld, Computerworld 100, Digital News, IT Casebook, Network World, On-line World Australia, PC World, Publishing Essentials, Reseller, WebMaster; Austria: Computerwelt Osterreich, Networks Austria, PC Tip; Belarus: PC World Belarus; Belgium: Data News; Brazil: Annuário de Informática, Computerworld Brazil, Connections, Super Game Power, Macworld, PC Player, PC World Brazil, Publish Brazil, Reseller News; Bulgaria: Computerworld Bulgaria, Networkworld/Bulgaria, PC & MacWorld Bulgaria; Canada: CIO Canada, Client/Server World, ComputerWorld Canada, InfoCanada, Network World Canada; Chile: Computerworld Chile, PC World Chile; Colombia: Computerworld Colombia, PC World Colombia; Costa Rica: PC World Centro America; The Czech and Slovak Republics: Computerworld Czechoslovakia, Elektronika Czechoslovakia, Macworld Czech Republic, PC World Czechoslovakia; Denmark: Communications World, Computerworld Danmark, Macworld Danmark, PC Privat Danmark, PC World Danmark, PC World Danmark Supplements, TECH World; Dominican Republic: PC World Republica Dominicana; Ecuador: PC World Ecuador; Egypt: Computerworld Middle East, PC World Middle East; El Salvador: PC World Centro America; Finland: MikroPC, Tietoverkko, Tietoviikko; France: Distributique, Golden, Hebdo-Distributique, Info PC, Le Guide du Monde Informatique, Le Monde Informatique, Reseaux & Telecoms; Germany: Computer Partner, Computerwoche, Computerwoche Extra, Computerwoche Focus, I/M Information Management, Macwelt, PC Welt; Greece: GamePro, Multimedia World; Guatemala: PC World Centro America; Honduras: PC World Centro America; Hong Kong: Computerworld Hong Kong, PCWorld Hong Kong, Publish in Asia; Hungary: ABCD CD-ROM, Computerworld Szamitastechnika, PC & Mac World Hungary, PC-X Magazine; Iceland: Tolvuheimur/PC World Island; India: Information Systems Computerworld, PC World India, Publish in Asia; Indonesia: InfoKomputer PC World, Komputek Computerworld, Publish in Asia; Israel: People & Computers; Italy: Computerworld Italia, Computerworld Italia Special Editions, Macworld Italia, Networking Italia, PC Shopping, PC World Italia, PC World/Walt Disney; Japan: DTP World, HP Open World Japan, Macworld Japan, Nikkei Personal Computing, Open World Japan, OS/2 World Japan, SunWorld Japan, Windows World Japan; Kenya: East African Computer News; Korea: Hi-Tech Information/Computerworld, Macworld Korea, PC World Korea; Macedonia: PC World Macedonia; Malaysia: Computerworld Malaysia, PC World Malaysia, Publish in Asia; Mexico: Computerworld Mexico, Macworld, PC World Mexico; Myanmar: PC World Myanmar; Netherlands: Computer! Totaal, LAN Magazine, LanWorld Buyers Guide, Macworld, Net Magazine, Totaal! Beurskrant; New Zealand: Absolute Beginner's Guide, Computer Buyer, Computer Industry Directory, Computerworld New Zealand, MTB, Network World, PC World New Zealand; Nicaragua: PC World Centro America; Nigeria: PC World Nigeria; Norway: Computerworld Norge, Computerworld Privat (Datamagasinet), CW Rapport Norge, IDG's KURSGUIDE, Macworld Norge, Multimediaworld, PC World Ekspress, PC World Nettverk, PC World Norge, PC World's Produktguide, Windows World Spesial; Pakistan: Computerworld Pakistan, PC World Pakistan; Panama: PC World Panama; P. R. of China: China Computer Users, China Computerworld, China Infoworld, China Telecom World Weekly, Computer & Communication, Electronic Design China, Electronics Today, Electronics Weekly, Game Camp, Game Soft, Network World China, PC World China, Popular Computer Weekly, Software Weekly, Software World, Telecom World; Peru: Computerworld Peru, PC World Profesional Peru, PC World Peru; Poland: Computerworld Poland, Computerworld Special Report, Macworld, Networld, PC World Komputer; Philippines: Computerworld Philippines, PC World Philippines, Publish in Asia; Portugal: Cerebro/PC World, Computerworld/Correio Informático, Dealer World Portugal, Mac*In/PC*In, Multimedia World Portugal; Puerto Rico: PC World Puerto Rico; Romania: Computerworld Romania, PC World Romania, Telecom Romania; Russia: Computerworld Russia, Mir PK, Sety; Singapore: Computerworld Singapore, PC World Singapore, Publish in Asia; Slovenia: MONITOR; South Africa: Computing S.A., InfoWorld S.A., Network World S.A., Software World; Spain: Computerworld Espa-a, COMUNICACIONES WORLD, Dealer World, Macworld Espa-a, PC World Espa-a; Sweden: CAP&Design, Computer Sweden, Corporate Computing, MacWorld, Maxi Data, MikroDatorn, Nätverk & Kommunikation, PC/Aktiv, PC World, Windows World; Switzerland: Computerworld Schweiz, Macworld Schweiz, PCtip; Taiwan: Computerworld Taiwan, Macworld Taiwan, PC World Taiwan, Publish Taiwan, Windows World; Thailand: Thai Computerworld, Publish in Asia; Turkey: Computerworld Turkiye, MACWORLD Turkiye, PC WORLD Turkiye; Ukraine: Computerworld Kiev, Computers & Software, Multimedia World, PC World Ukraine; United Kingdom: Acorn User, Amiga Action, Amiga Computing, Appletalk, Computing, GamePro, Macworld, Network News, Parents and Computers, PC Advisor, PC Home, PSX Pro UK, The WEB; United States: Cable in the Classroom, CD Review, CIO Magazine, Computerworld, Computerworld Client/Server Journal, Digital Video Magazine, DOS World, Federal Computer Week, GamePro, InfoWorld, I-Way, JavaWorld, Macworld, Multimedia World, Netscape World Online, Network World, PC Entertainment, PC World, Publish, SunWorld Online, SWATPro Magazine, Video Event, WebMaster; Uruguay: PC World Uruguay; Venezuela: Computerworld Venezuela, PC World Venezuela; and Vietnam: PC World Vietnam.

*Every maranGraphics book represents
the extraordinary vision and commitment of a unique family:
the Maran family of Toronto, Canada.*

Back Row (from left to right): *Sherry Maran, Rob Maran, Richard Maran, Maxine Maran, Jill Maran.*
Front Row (from left to right): *Judy Maran, Ruth Maran.*

Richard Maran is the company founder and its inspirational leader. He developed maranGraphics' proprietary communication technology called "visual grammar." This book is built on that technology—empowering readers with the easiest and quickest way to learn about computers.

Ruth Maran is the Author and Architect—a role Richard established that now bears Ruth's distinctive touch. She creates the words and visual structure that are the basis for the books.

Judy Maran is the Project Manager. She works with Ruth, Richard and the highly talented maranGraphics illustrators, designers and editors to transform Ruth's material into its final form.

Rob Maran is the Technical and Production Specialist. He makes sure the state-of-the-art technology used to create these books always performs as it should.

Sherry Maran manages the Reception, Order Desk and any number of areas that require immediate attention and a helping hand.

Jill Maran is a jack-of-all-trades who works in the Accounting and Human Resources department.

Maxine Maran is the Business Manager and family sage. She maintains order in the business and family—and keeps everything running smoothly.

Oh, and three other family members are seated on the sofa. These graphic disk characters help make it fun and easy to learn about computers. They're part of the extended maranGraphics family.

Credits

Author:
Ruth Maran

Technical Updates:
Robert Maran
Paul Whitehead

Copy Development Director:
Kelleigh Wing

Copy Developer:
Jason M. Brown

Project Manager:
Judy Maran

Editors:
Raquel Scott
Janice Boyer
Michelle Kirchner
James Menzies
Frances LoPresti
Emmet Mellow

**Layout Designers &
Illustrators:**
Jamie Bell
Treena Lees

**3-Dimensional Computers &
Illustrations:**
Russ Marini

Illustrators:
Jeff Jones
Peter Grecco

Indexer:
Raquel Scott

Permissions Coordinator:
Jenn Hillman

Post Production:
Robert Maran

Editorial Support:
Michael Roney

Acknowledgments

Thanks to the dedicated staff of maranGraphics, including
Jamie Bell, Cathy Benn, Janice Boyer, Jason M. Brown,
Francisco Ferreira, Peter Grecco, Jenn Hillman, Jeff Jones,
Michelle Kirchner, Wanda Lawrie, Treena Lees, Frances LoPresti,
Michael W. MacDonald, Jill Maran, Judy Maran, Maxine Maran,
Robert Maran, Sherry Maran, Russ Marini, Emmet Mellow,
James Menzies, Raquel Scott, Roxanne Van Damme,
Paul Whitehead and Kelleigh Wing.

Finally, to Richard Maran who originated the easy-to-use
graphic format of this guide. Thank you for your inspiration
and guidance.

Screen Shot Permissions

Table of Contents

CHAPTER 4

STORAGE DEVICES

CHAPTER 5

PORTABLE COMPUTERS

CHAPTER 6

APPLICATION SOFTWARE

Table of Contents

HARDWARE AND SOFTWARE

Hardware and software are the two basic parts of a computer system.

HARDWARE

Hardware is any part of a computer system you can see or touch.

Peripheral

A peripheral is any piece of hardware attached to a computer, such as a printer.

SOFTWARE

Software is a set of electronic instructions that tell a computer what to do. You cannot see or touch software, but you can see and touch the packaging the software comes in.

Application Software

Application software allows you to accomplish specific tasks. Popular application software includes Microsoft® Word and Intuit Quicken.

Operating System Software

Operating system software controls the overall activity of a computer. Most new computers come with the Windows 98 operating system software.

There are many ways to get help when using new hardware and software.

Documentation

Hardware and software should include documentation that tells you how to set up and use the product. Many software packages also come with a built-in help feature. You can also check local book stores for manuals with detailed, step-by-step instructions.

Call the Experts

If you have questions about setting up or using new hardware or software, try calling the store where you purchased the product.

Classes

Colleges and computer stores often offer computer courses. Many communities also have computer clubs where you can ask questions and exchange ideas.

HOW COMPUTERS WORK

A computer collects, processes, stores and outputs information.

INPUT

An input device lets you communicate with a computer. You can use input devices to enter information and issue commands. A keyboard, mouse and joystick are input devices.

PROCESS

The Central Processing Unit (CPU) is the main chip in a computer. The CPU processes instructions, performs calculations and manages the flow of information through a computer system. The CPU communicates with input, output and storage devices to perform tasks.

STORE

A storage device is used to place information on storage media. The computer uses information stored on the storage media to perform tasks. Popular examples of storage devices include a hard drive, floppy drive, recordable CD-ROM drive, tape drive and DVD-ROM drive.

OUTPUT

An output device lets a computer communicate with you. These devices display information on a screen, create printed copies or generate sound. A monitor, printer and speakers are output devices.

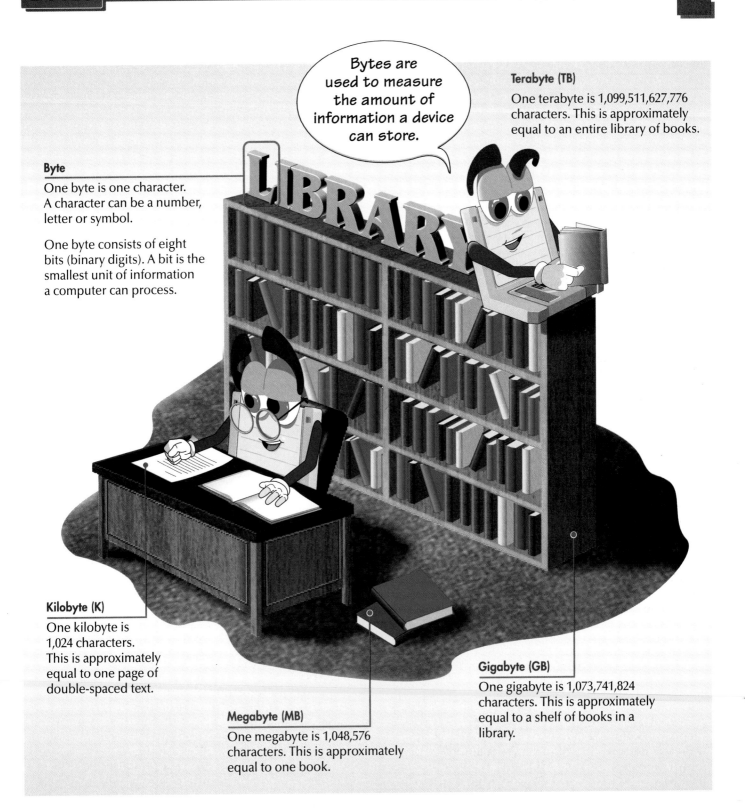

Bytes are used to measure the amount of information a device can store.

Terabyte (TB)
One terabyte is 1,099,511,627,776 characters. This is approximately equal to an entire library of books.

Byte
One byte is one character. A character can be a number, letter or symbol.

One byte consists of eight bits (binary digits). A bit is the smallest unit of information a computer can process.

Kilobyte (K)
One kilobyte is 1,024 characters. This is approximately equal to one page of double-spaced text.

Megabyte (MB)
One megabyte is 1,048,576 characters. This is approximately equal to one book.

Gigabyte (GB)
One gigabyte is 1,073,741,824 characters. This is approximately equal to a shelf of books in a library.

TYPES OF COMPUTER SYSTEMS

PC (PERSONAL COMPUTER)

A PC is a computer designed to meet the needs of a single person and usually refers to IBM-compatible computers. PCs are found in many businesses and are popular for home use.

There are several types of computer systems.

MACINTOSH

Macintosh computers are found in many homes and are very popular in the graphics, publishing and multimedia industries. The Macintosh was the first home computer that offered a graphical display.

MAINFRAME

A mainframe is a computer that can process and store large amounts of information and support many users at the same time. A terminal, consisting of a keyboard and monitor, is used to input and output information on a mainframe.

SET-TOP BOX

A set-top box is a computer device that connects to your television. Set-top boxes allow you to use your telephone line or cable connection to browse the Internet and exchange electronic mail on your television.

A TYPICAL COMPUTER

A typical computer system consists of several parts.

Computer Case
A computer case contains all the major components of a computer system.

Monitor
A monitor is a device that displays text and images generated by the computer.

Printer
A printer is a device that produces a paper copy of documents you create on the computer.

Modem
A modem is a device that lets computers communicate through telephone lines. A modem can be found inside or outside the computer case.

Keyboard
A keyboard is a device that lets you type information and instructions into a computer.

Mouse
A mouse is a handheld device that lets you select and move items on the screen.

Power Supply

A power supply changes normal household electricity into electricity that a computer can use.

Hard Drive

A hard drive is the primary device that a computer uses to store information.

Expansion Card

An expansion card lets you add new features to a computer. For example, an expansion card can give a computer the ability to record and play sound.

Expansion Slot

An expansion slot is a socket on the motherboard. An expansion card plugs into an expansion slot.

Motherboard

A motherboard is the main circuit board of a computer. All electrical components plug into the motherboard.

All computers contain the same basic components.

Floppy Drive

A floppy drive stores and retrieves information on floppy disks.

Drive Bay

A drive bay is a space inside the computer case where a hard drive, floppy drive, CD-ROM drive or DVD-ROM drive sits.

CD-ROM or DVD-ROM Drive

A CD-ROM drive reads information stored on compact discs (CDs). A DVD-ROM drive reads information stored on CDs and digital versatile discs (DVDs).

Random Access Memory (RAM)

RAM temporarily stores information inside a computer. This information is lost when you turn off the computer.

Central Processing Unit (CPU)

A CPU is the main chip in a computer. The CPU processes instructions, performs calculations and manages the flow of information through a computer.

COMPUTER CASE

A computer case contains all the major components of a computer system.

Desktop Case

A desktop case usually sits on a desk, under a monitor.

Tower Case

A tower case usually sits on the floor. This provides more desk space, but can be less convenient for inserting and removing floppy disks and CD-ROM discs. Tower cases come in different sizes.

PORTABLE

A portable is a small, lightweight computer that you can easily transport. A portable has a built-in keyboard and screen.

ALL-IN-ONE CASE

An all-in-one case contains a monitor, disk drive, CD-ROM drive and speakers in a single unit.

POWER SUPPLY

A power supply changes the alternating current (AC) that comes from an outlet to the direct current (DC) that a computer can use.

A fan inside the power supply prevents the parts inside a computer from overheating.

The capacity of a power supply is measured in watts. An average computer uses up to 200 watts, whereas an average light bulb uses 60 watts.

PROTECT YOUR EQUIPMENT

Changes in electrical power can damage equipment and information.

Surge Protector

A surge protector, or surge suppressor, guards a computer against surges. A surge is a fluctuation in power. These fluctuations happen most often during storms.

UPS

An Uninterruptible Power Supply (UPS) protects a computer from a loss of power. A UPS contains a battery that stores electrical power. If the power fails, the battery can run the computer for a short time so you can save your information.

> A port is a connector at the back of a computer where you plug in an external device such as a printer or modem. This allows instructions and data to flow between the computer and the device.

Parallel Port

A parallel port has 25 holes. This type of port is known as a female connector. A parallel port connects a printer or tape drive.

A computer internally labels each parallel port with the letters LPT. The first parallel port is named LPT1, the second parallel port is named LPT2, and so on.

Monitor Port

A monitor port connects a monitor.

Serial Port

A serial port has either 9 or 25 pins. This type of port is known as a male connector. A serial port connects a mouse or modem.

A computer internally labels each serial port with the letters COM. The first serial port is named COM1, the second serial port is named COM2, and so on.

Keyboard Port

A keyboard port connects a keyboard. A keyboard port can come in two sizes.

Game Port

A game port connects a joystick.

USB Port

Universal Serial Bus (USB) is a type of port that allows you to connect up to 127 devices using only one port. For example, you can use a USB port to connect a printer, modem, joystick and scanner to your computer. Most new computers come with two USB ports.

EXPANSION CARD

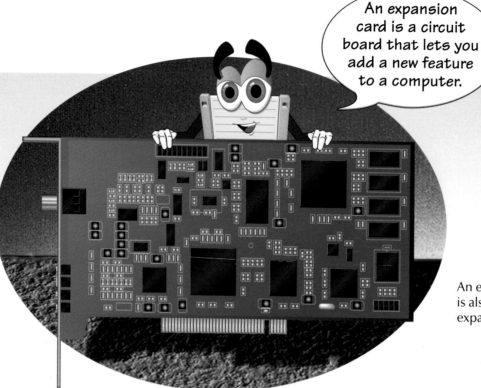

An expansion card is a circuit board that lets you add a new feature to a computer.

An expansion card is also called an expansion board.

EXPANSION SLOT

An expansion slot is a socket where you plug in an expansion card.

The number of expansion slots your computer has indicates how many features you can add to the computer. Before you buy a computer, make sure it has enough empty expansion slots for your future needs.

CONNECT DEVICES

Some expansion cards are accessible from the back of a computer. These expansion cards contain ports where you can plug in devices. For example, you can plug speakers into a sound card to hear the sound generated by the computer.

TYPES OF EXPANSION CARDS

A computer usually comes with one or more expansion cards.

Video

A video card generates the images displayed on the monitor.

Modem

A modem card lets computers exchange information through telephone lines.

Sound

A sound card lets a computer play and record high-quality sound.

Networking

A network interface card lets connected computers share information and equipment.

CONSIDERATIONS

Cost

The cost of a computer depends on your needs. You can purchase a basic home computer for under $1,000. If you want a computer better able to handle complex tasks, such as running multimedia applications, you will need to spend more money.

There are many aspects to consider when purchasing a new computer.

In most cases, a monitor is not included in the price of a computer.

Brand-name and Clone Computers

When purchasing a new computer, you can choose either a brand-name or a clone computer. Brand-name computers are made by large manufacturers, such as IBM or Dell. Clone computers are made by independent manufacturers. Clone computers function exactly like brand-name computers, but are usually less expensive.

After-sale Service

You should make sure the computer you purchase comes with after-sale service. After-sale service should include a one or two-year warranty on computer parts and labor, as well as telephone technical support.

Upgrading usually refers to replacing an old or obsolete component with a newer component to improve the efficiency of the computer. Upgrading can also include adding a new component, such as a tape drive or DVD-ROM drive, to increase the capabilities of the computer.

CONSIDERATIONS

Cost

You should always determine the cost of an upgrade before performing the upgrade. If you are planning a major upgrade, such as replacing the motherboard or CPU, it may be less expensive to purchase a new computer.

Effective Upgrades

Increasing the amount of memory in a computer is one of the most effective upgrades you can perform. Doubling the existing memory in a computer can significantly increase the performance of the computer.

INPUT AND OUTPUT

A mouse is a handheld pointing device that lets you select and move items on your screen.

A mouse can come in various shapes, colors and sizes.

USE THE MOUSE

Resting your hand on the mouse, use your thumb and two rightmost fingers to move the mouse on the desk. Use your two remaining fingers to press the mouse buttons.

When you move the mouse on your desk, the pointer on the screen moves in the same direction. The pointer assumes different shapes (example: ⌐ or I) depending on its location on the screen and the task you are performing.

There are four common mouse actions.

Click

A click often selects an item on the screen. To click, press and release the left mouse button.

Drag and Drop

Dragging and dropping makes it easy to move an item on the screen. Position the pointer over an item on the screen and then press and hold down the left mouse button. Still holding down the button, move the pointer to where you want to place the item and then release the button.

Double-click

A double-click often opens a document or starts a program. To double-click, quickly press and release the left mouse button twice.

Right-click

A right-click often displays a list of commands on the screen. To right-click, press and release the right mouse button.

LEFT-HANDED USERS

If you are left-handed, you can switch the functions of the left and right mouse buttons to make the mouse easier to use. For example, to click an item, you would press the right button instead of the left.

WHEELED MOUSE

A wheeled mouse has a wheel between the left and right mouse buttons. You can often use this wheel to scroll through information or zoom in and out. The Microsoft IntelliMouse is a popular example of a wheeled mouse.

MOUSE PAD

Hard plastic mouse pads tend to attract less dirt and provide a smoother surface than fabric-covered mouse pads.

> A mouse pad provides a smooth surface for moving a mouse and reduces the amount of dirt that enters the mouse.

You can buy mouse pads displaying interesting designs or pictures at most computer stores. Some mouse pads have built-in wrist support for increased comfort.

CLEAN THE MOUSE

You should occasionally remove and clean the ball inside the mouse. Make sure you also remove dust and dirt from the inside to help ensure smooth motion of the mouse.

CORDLESS MOUSE

A cordless mouse runs on a battery and reduces the clutter on your desk by eliminating the mouse cord. When you move the mouse on your desk, the mouse sends signals through the air to your computer, the same way a remote control sends signals to a television.

OTHER POINTING DEVICES

Joystick

A joystick helps you control the movement of people and objects in many computer games. Joysticks are used for arcade-type computer games because they let you move quickly and accurately in any direction.

Touchpad

A touchpad is a surface that is sensitive to pressure and motion. When you move your fingertip across the pad, the pointer on the screen moves in the same direction.

Trackball

A trackball is an upside-down mouse that remains stationary on your desk. You roll the ball with your fingers or palm to move the pointer on the screen. A trackball is a great alternative to a mouse when you have limited desk space.

KEYBOARD

Most keyboards have 101 keys. Your keyboard may look different from the keyboard shown here.

The keys on a keyboard let you enter information and instructions into a computer.

Escape Key

You can press **Esc** to quit a task you are performing.

Caps Lock and Shift Keys

These keys let you enter text in uppercase (ABC) and lowercase (abc) letters.

Press **Caps Lock** to change the case of all letters you type. Press the key again to return to the original case.

Press **Shift** in combination with another key to type an uppercase letter.

Function Keys

These keys let you quickly perform specific tasks. For example, in many programs you can press **F1** to display help information.

Ctrl and Alt Keys

You can use the **Ctrl** or **Alt** key in combination with another key to perform a specific task. For example, in some programs you can press **Ctrl** and **S** to save a document.

Windows Key

You can press the **Windows** key to quickly display the Start menu when using the Windows 95, 98 or NT operating systems.

Spacebar

You can press the **Spacebar** to insert a blank space.

Backspace Key

You can press **Backspace** to remove the character to the left of the cursor.

Delete Key

You can press **Delete** to remove the character to the right of the cursor.

Status Lights

These lights indicate whether the **Num Lock** or **Caps Lock** features are on or off.

Numeric Keypad

When the **Num Lock** light is on, you can use the number keys (0 through 9) to enter numbers. When the **Num Lock** light is off, you can use these keys to move the cursor around the screen. To turn the light on or off, press **Num Lock**.

Application Key

You can press the **Application** key to quickly display the shortcut menu for an item on your screen.

Enter Key

You can press **Enter** to tell the computer to carry out a task. In a word processing program, press this key to start a new paragraph.

Arrow Keys

These keys let you move the cursor around the screen.

A printer produces a paper copy of the information displayed on the screen.

You can buy a printer that produces black-and-white or color images.

You can use a printer to produce letters, invoices, newsletters, transparencies, labels, packing slips and much more.

CHOOSE A PRINTER

There are several factors to consider when buying a printer.

■ Make sure the printer will work with your computer and software.

■ Check the size and type of paper the printer accepts. Some printers can print on large sheets of paper.

■ Check the cost of materials such as ink and paper.

■ Check the amount of paper the printer tray can hold.

■ If you want to print on envelopes, make sure the printer will accept envelopes.

PRINTER SPEED

The speed of a printer determines how quickly it can print the pages you selected. Speed is measured in pages per minute (ppm). A higher speed results in faster output.

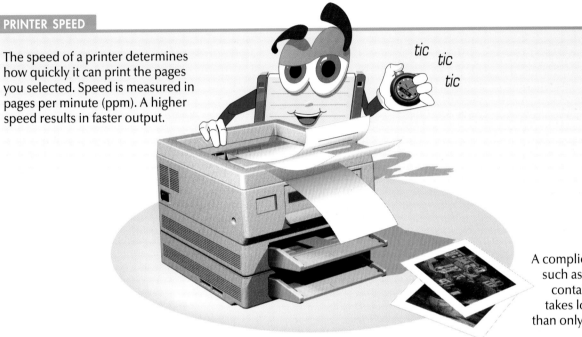

tic tic tic

A complicated page, such as a page that contains graphics, takes longer to print than only text.

PRINTER RESOLUTION

The resolution of a printer determines the quality of the images it can produce. A higher resolution results in sharper, more detailed images.

Printer resolution is measured in dots per inch (dpi). Generally, a resolution of 600 dpi is acceptable for most office documents. 1200 dpi printers are better for printing graphics.

600 dpi

1200 dpi

INK-JET PRINTER

An ink-jet printer has a print head that sprays ink through small holes onto a page.

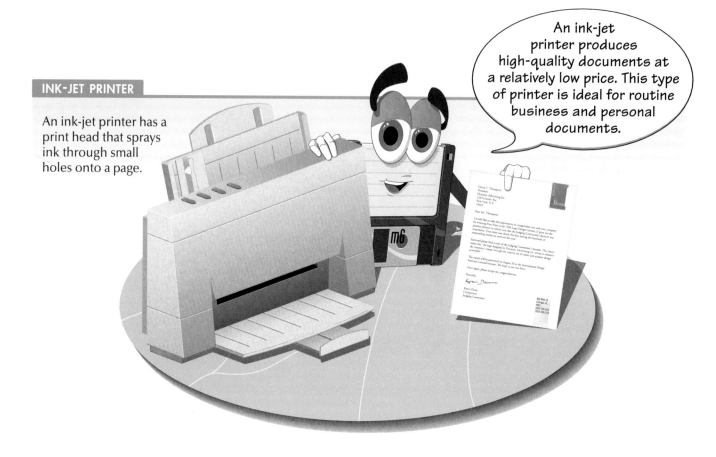

An ink-jet printer produces high-quality documents at a relatively low price. This type of printer is ideal for routine business and personal documents.

Speed

Most ink-jet printers produce images at a speed of 0.5 to 4 pages per minute (ppm).

Resolution

The resolution, or quality, of the images produced by an ink-jet printer ranges from 180 to 720 dots per inch (dpi).

Ink

Ink-jet printers use ink stored in cartridges. When the ink runs out, you replace the cartridge.

Many ink cartridges have an expiry date on them. Before you buy a new cartridge, you should make sure it has not expired.

Paper

Ink-jet printers accept 8 ½ by 11-inch paper. Some ink-jet printers accept larger paper sizes. Ink-jet printers also accept envelopes, labels and transparencies. Make sure you buy items designed specifically for use with ink-jet printers.

Color

Color ink-jet printers are very popular because they are less expensive than color laser printers and still produce high-quality color images.

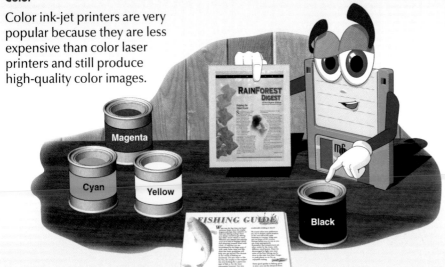

A color ink-jet printer sprays cyan, magenta, yellow and black ink to create images on a page. Lower-cost color ink-jet printers create black by mixing the cyan, magenta and yellow ink. The best color images come from printers that offer black as a separate color.

Some ink-jet printers use more than four colors of ink, which allows you to print even higher-quality color images.

LASER PRINTER

A laser printer is a high-speed printer that is ideal for business and personal documents and for proofing professional graphics work.

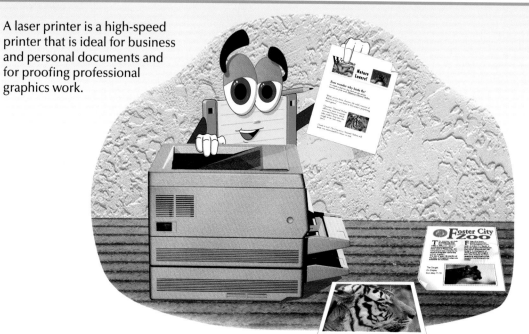

A laser printer works like a photocopier to produce high-quality images on a page.

Speed

Most laser printers produce images at a speed of 4 to 20 pages per minute (ppm).

All laser printers have a Central Processing Unit (CPU) that processes instructions and manages the flow of information in the printer. The CPU speed is a major factor in determining how fast a laser printer operates. The faster the CPU speed, the faster the printer will produce images.

Resolution

The resolution, or quality, of the images produced by a laser printer ranges from 300 to 1200 dots per inch (dpi).

Paper

All laser printers can print on 8 ½ by 11-inch paper, envelopes, labels and transparencies. Make sure you buy items designed specifically for use with laser printers.

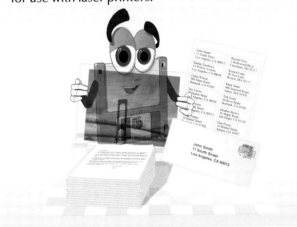

Ink

Like photocopiers, laser printers use a fine powdered ink, called toner, which comes in a cartridge. When the toner runs out, you buy a new cartridge.

Color

You can buy laser printers that produce color images. A color laser printer is more expensive than a color ink jet printer, but it produces superior output.

Memory

Laser printers store pages in built-in memory before printing. A typical laser printer comes with 4 MB to 8 MB of memory.

Memory is important for laser printers that produce images at high resolutions, such as 1200 dpi. Memory is also important for laser printers that print on larger paper sizes and process complex print jobs.

Laser Printer Languages

A printer language is software that tells a printer how to print a document. There are two main types of laser printer languages—PCL and PostScript.

PCL

Most laser printers come with Printer Control Language (PCL). A PCL laser printer is less expensive, but does not offer the graphic capabilities of a PostScript printer. The PCL language is popular for routine office tasks.

PostScript

A PostScript laser printer can handle more complex documents that include various colors, graphics and fonts. The PostScript language is required by some programs used in the graphic arts industry.

OTHER TYPES OF PRINTERS

Dot-matrix Printer

A dot-matrix printer is the least expensive type of printer and produces low-quality images. Inside a dot-matrix printer, a print head containing small, blunt pins strikes an inked ribbon. This is ideal for printing on multipart forms that need an impact to print through multiple copies.

Solid Ink Printer

A solid ink printer produces high-quality color images at a relatively low price. This type of printer is ideal for producing crisp color images on regular paper and transparencies.

Dye Sublimation Printer

A dye sublimation printer is the most expensive type of printer and produces images that look like color photographs. Dye sublimation printers are also called thermal dye transfer printers.

Multifunction Printer

A multifunction printer can perform more than one task. This type of printer is often able to work as a fax machine, scanner and photocopier as well as a printer. Color multifunction printers are also available.

FONT

A font is a set of characters with a particular design and size. You can use different fonts to make documents more attractive and interesting.

Most printers come with a few built-in fonts, called resident fonts. Resident fonts print faster than the fonts stored on your computer.

TrueType Font

A TrueType font generates characters using mathematical formulas. You can change the size of a TrueType font without distorting the font. A TrueType font will print exactly as it appears on the screen.

Bitmapped Font

A bitmapped font stores each character as a picture made up of a pattern of dots. If you change the size of a bitmapped font, the font may become distorted.

PRINT BUFFER AND SPOOLER

A computer can send data faster than a printer can accept and process the data. A print spooler or print buffer acts like a dam, holding the data and then releasing it at a speed the printer can handle.

Print Buffer

A print buffer is a section of memory in a printer that stores information you selected to print. When the buffer is full, the computer must wait before sending more data to the printer.

Print Spooler

A print spooler is a program on your computer that stores information you selected to print.

A print spooler can store more information than a print buffer and lets you continue using your computer without having to wait for a document to finish printing. Windows comes with a built-in print spooler.

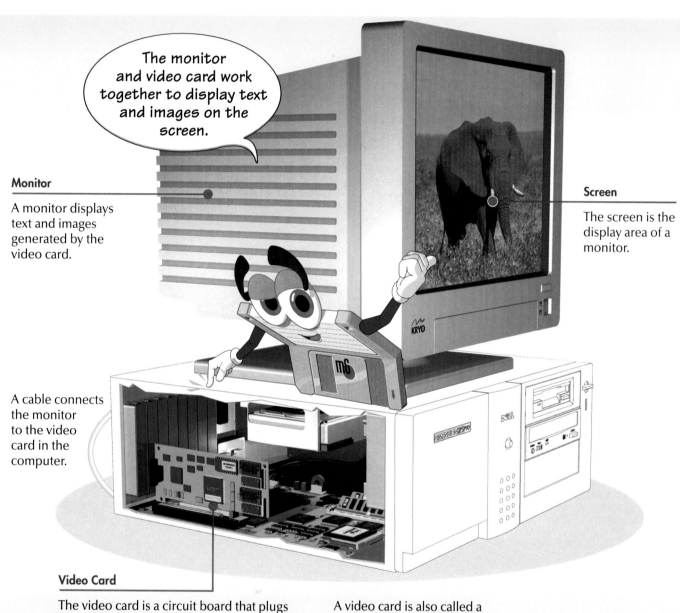

The monitor and video card work together to display text and images on the screen.

Monitor

A monitor displays text and images generated by the video card.

Screen

The screen is the display area of a monitor.

A cable connects the monitor to the video card in the computer.

Video Card

The video card is a circuit board that plugs into an expansion slot inside the computer. The video card translates instructions from the computer to a form the monitor can understand.

A video card is also called a video adapter, video board, graphics adapter, graphics board or graphics card.

CHOOSE A MONITOR

Size

The size of a monitor is measured diagonally across the screen. Common monitor sizes are 14, 15, 17 and 21 inches. Larger monitors are more expensive and are ideal for desktop publishing and working with graphics or large spreadsheets.

Manufacturers usually advertise the diagonal measurement of the picture tube inside the monitor, which is greater than the actual viewing area. Make sure you ask for the size of the viewing area.

Flat-panel

A flat-panel monitor uses Liquid Crystal Display (LCD), which is the same type of display found in most digital wristwatches. In the past, flat-panel screens were only used on portable computers, but now full-size flat-panel monitors are available for desktop computers.

Flat-panel monitors are more expensive than desktop monitors, but are lighter, take up less desk space and use less electricity.

Dot Pitch

The dot pitch is the distance between tiny dots on a screen. The dot pitch determines the sharpness of images on the screen.

The smaller the dot pitch, the crisper the images. Select a monitor with a dot pitch of 0.28 mm or less.

CHOOSE A MONITOR (CONTINUED)

Refresh Rate

The refresh rate determines the speed that a monitor redraws, or updates, images. The higher the refresh rate, the less flicker on the screen. This helps reduce eye strain.

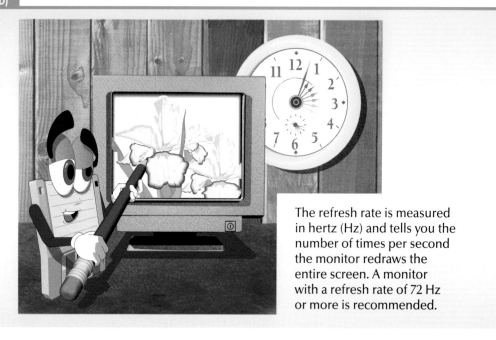

The refresh rate is measured in hertz (Hz) and tells you the number of times per second the monitor redraws the entire screen. A monitor with a refresh rate of 72 Hz or more is recommended.

Controls

Monitors have controls to adjust the brightness, contrast and other features of the images displayed on the screen. You can find controls on the screen or on the monitor.

Tilt-and-swivel Base

A tilt-and-swivel base lets you adjust the angle of the screen. This lets you reduce the glare from overhead lighting and view the screen more comfortably.

Electromagnetic Radiation

Any device that uses electricity produces Electromagnetic Radiation (EMR). You can protect yourself from potentially harmful effects by remaining a safe distance away from electrical devices.

Monitors emit EMR, but you can minimize the risk by buying a monitor that meets MPR II guidelines. The MPR II guidelines define acceptable levels of EMR.

You can further minimize the risk by turning off the monitor when it is not in use. Also avoid sitting near the sides or back of a monitor, which emit more EMR than the front.

Energy Star

The Environmental Protection Agency (EPA) developed an energy-saving guideline called ENERGY STAR to reduce wasted energy and the pollution it causes.

When you do not use an ENERGY STAR computer for a period of time, the monitor and computer enter an energy-saving sleep mode. You awaken the computer by moving the mouse or pressing a key on the keyboard.

MONITOR TIPS

Screen Saver

A screen saver is a moving picture or pattern that appears on the screen when you do not use a computer for a period of time.

Screen savers were originally designed to prevent screen burn, which occurs when an image appears in a fixed position for a period of time.

Today's monitors are designed to prevent screen burn, but people still use screen savers for entertainment.

Windows provides several screen savers. You can purchase more sophisticated screen savers at most computer stores.

Using a process called Webcasting, you can also use screen savers that display customized, up-to-the-minute information. This information is transferred to your computer from the Internet.

Glare Filter

A glare filter fits over the front of a monitor to reduce the amount of light reflected off the computer screen. This helps reduce eye strain.

Most glare filters also help block the radiation coming from the front of the monitor.

VIDEO CARD MEMORY

A video card has memory chips. These chips temporarily store information before sending it to the monitor.

Most computers require at least 2 MB of video card memory.

VRAM

Video Random Access Memory (VRAM) is a type of memory specifically designed for video cards. VRAM is ideal for displaying complex graphics.

Extended Data Out Dynamic RAM (EDO DRAM) and Window RAM (WRAM) are two other types of video card memory.

AGP

An Accelerated Graphics Port (AGP) video card uses an AGP bus to communicate directly with your computer's main memory. This allows you to quickly display complex graphics on your monitor.

AGP is specially designed to meet the high demands of displaying 3-D graphics.

RESOLUTION

Resolution is measured by the number of horizontal and vertical pixels. A pixel is the smallest element on the screen. Pixel is short for picture element.

Resolution determines the amount of information a monitor can display.

A multisync monitor lets you adjust the resolution to suit your needs. Other monitors can display only one resolution.

640 x 480

800 x 600

1,024 x 768

1,280 x 1,024

Lower resolutions display larger images so you can see information more clearly.

Higher resolutions display smaller images so you can display more information at once.

VGA

Video Graphics Array (VGA) monitors display 16 colors at a resolution of 640 x 480. This is the minimum standard for computer systems.

SVGA

Super Video Graphics Array (SVGA) monitors display more colors and higher resolutions than VGA monitors. Most new computer systems offer SVGA.

The number of colors a monitor can display determines how realistic images appear on a screen. More colors result in more realistic images.

16 Colors (4-bit color)

Choppy-looking images.

256 Colors (8-bit color)

Ideal for most home, business and game applications.

65,536 Colors (16-bit color)

Ideal for video and desktop publishing applications. Unless you are a trained professional, it is difficult to distinguish between 16-bit and 24-bit color.

16,777,216 Colors (24-bit color)

Ideal for photographic work. This setting is also called true color because it displays more colors than the human eye can distinguish.

A modem lets computers exchange information through telephone lines.

A modem translates computer information into a form that can transmit over phone lines.

Phone Line

You do not need a separate phone line to use a modem. You can use the same phone line for telephone and modem calls. If your telephone and modem share the same line, make sure you turn off the call waiting feature when using your modem, since this feature could disrupt the modem connection.

The receiving modem translates the information it receives into a form the computer can understand.

MODEM APPLICATIONS

Connect to the Internet

A modem lets you connect to the Internet and online services such as America Online and AT&T WorldNet. This lets you access a vast amount of information and meet thousands of people with similar interests.

Exchange Information

When traveling or at home, you can use a modem to access information stored on the network at work. You can send and receive electronic messages (e-mail) and work with office files.

Send and Receive Faxes

Most modems can send and receive faxes. With a fax modem, you can create a document on your computer and then fax the document to another computer or fax machine.

When a computer receives a fax, the document appears on the screen. You can review and print the document, but you cannot edit the document unless you have Optical Character Recognition (OCR) software.

Internal Modem

An internal modem is a circuit board that plugs into an expansion slot in a computer. This type of modem is generally less expensive than an external modem, but is more difficult to set up.

You can see the edge of an internal modem at the back of a computer.

External Modem

An external modem is a small box that plugs into the back of a computer. An external modem takes up room on your desk, but you can use this type of modem with more than one computer.

Status lights on the modem tell you about the current transmission. For example, the RD light is on when the modem is receiving data.

If you are using an external modem with an older computer, make sure the computer uses a 16550 UART chip. This will ensure that the computer can handle current modem speeds. A UART chip controls the flow of information to and from the modem.

MODEM SPEED

The speed of a modem determines how fast it can send and receive information through telephone lines.

Modem speed is measured in bits per second (bps). You should buy a modem with a speed of at least 33,600 bps.

Modem speeds of 56,000 bps are now available.

Modem speed is also measured in kilobits per second (Kbps). For example, a 33,600 bps modem is also referred to as a 33.6 Kbps modem.

Buy the fastest modem you can afford. Faster modems transfer information more quickly. This will save you time and reduce online service charges and long distance charges.

Line Quality

The speed at which information transfers depends on the quality of the phone line. For example, a modem with a speed of 33,600 bps may not reach that speed if the phone line quality is poor.

Modem Standards

Modem standards ensure that modems made by different manufacturers can communicate with each other. V.90 is the new standard for 56 Kbps modems. A V.90 modem can transfer data to a computer at a speed of 56,000 bps, but can only send data at a speed of 33,600 bps.

HOW MODEMS COMMUNICATE

Communications Program

A modem needs a communications program to manage the transmission of information with another modem. This type of program usually comes packaged with a modem.

Handshake

Before exchanging information, modems perform a handshake just as two people shake hands to greet each other. A handshake establishes how the modems will exchange information.

Modems must use the same speed when exchanging information. A fast modem can talk to a slower modem, but they will communicate at the slower speed. You may find that some online services use lower speed modems.

Online

You are online when your modem has successfully connected to another modem. This means the modems are ready and able to exchange information. When your modem is not connected to another modem, you are offline.

DATA COMPRESSION

A modem can compress, or squeeze together, data sent to another modem to speed the transfer of data. The speed of data transfer depends on the type of file being sent. For example, a text file will compress significantly more than a graphics file.

When the information reaches its intended destination, the receiving modem decompresses the information.

A modem uses error control to ensure that information reliably reaches its destination.

ISDN

Instead of using a modem and a regular phone line, some companies use an Integrated Services Digital Network (ISDN) line. ISDN is currently the best choice for a company that needs to connect several networked computers to the Internet.

ISDN transfers information between the Internet Service Provider (ISP) and a company about four times faster than a modem.

SOUND CARD

A sound card lets a computer play and record high-quality sound.

A sound card is a circuit board that plugs into an expansion slot in the computer.

A sound card is also called a sound board or audio card.

Speakers

You need speakers to hear the sound generated by a sound card. You should buy speakers with a built-in amplifier to strengthen the sound signal and improve the performance.

SOUND CARD APPLICATIONS

Games and Multimedia Presentations

A sound card lets you hear music, speech and sound effects during games and multimedia presentations.

Record Sounds

You can use a sound card to record music, speech and sound effects. You can then add the sounds to documents and presentations. You can also use a sound card to compose music on your computer.

SOUND CARD CONNECTIONS

You can see the edge of a sound card at the back of a computer. A sound card has a port and several jacks where you can plug in external devices.

The edge of your sound card may look different from the sound card shown here.

Joystick

This port lets you connect a joystick or a MIDI device such as a music keyboard.

Line In

This jack lets you connect a cassette or CD player to play music.

Spk Out

This jack lets you connect speakers or headphones to hear sound generated by a sound card.

Line Out

This jack lets you connect an amplifier to play sound through your home stereo.

Mic In

This jack lets you connect a microphone to record speech and other sounds.

SOUND CARD

Sampling Size and Rate

The sampling size and rate of a sound card determines the quality of the sound produced.

For good sound quality, buy a sound card with a 16-bit sampling size and a 44.1 KHz sampling rate.

If possible, listen to the sounds produced by various sound cards before making your purchase.

Sound Blaster

Make sure you buy a Sound Blaster compatible sound card to ensure your computer has full sound capabilities.

Full-duplex

A full-duplex sound card lets you talk and listen at the same time. When using a computer to have a conversation over the Internet, a full-duplex sound card lets people talk at the same time. With a half-duplex card, people must take turns talking.

MIDI

Musical Instrument Digital Interface (MIDI) is a set of instructions that allow computers and musical devices to exchange data. This lets you use a computer to play, record and edit music. Many musicians use MIDI to compose music on a computer.

A sound card that supports MIDI ensures that a computer can generate the sounds often found in games, CD-ROM titles and presentation packages.

> There are two ways a sound card can produce MIDI sound.

FM Synthesis

FM synthesis imitates the sounds of musical instruments and speech. This results in less realistic sound. FM synthesis is found on low to mid-range sound cards.

Wavetable Synthesis

Wavetable synthesis uses actual recordings of musical instruments and speech. This results in rich, realistic sound. Wavetable synthesis is found on high-quality sound cards.

A scanner is a device that reads graphics and text into a computer.

Scan Graphics

You can scan graphics such as photographs, drawings and logos into a computer. You can then use the graphics in documents, such as reports or newsletters.

Most scanners come with image editing software, which lets you change the appearance of a scanned graphic.

Scan Text

You can scan text to quickly enter documents into a computer. This lets you scan interesting paper documents and e-mail them to friends or colleagues. You can also scan office documents to store them on your computer for quick access.

Most scanners come with Optical Character Recognition (OCR) software. This software places scanned text into a document that can be edited in a word processor.

TYPES OF SCANNERS

Handheld Scanner

A handheld scanner is the least expensive type of scanner. A handheld scanner has a scanning width of approximately four inches and is ideal for copying small images, such as signatures, logos and small photographs.

Sheet-fed Scanner

A sheet-fed scanner produces more reliable scans than a handheld scanner and is less expensive and more compact than a flatbed scanner. A sheet-fed scanner can scan only single sheets of paper. If you want to scan a page from a book, you have to tear out the page.

Flatbed Scanner

A flatbed scanner is the most expensive and most versatile type of scanner. A flatbed scanner is ideal when you want to scan pages from a book without tearing out the pages.

COLOR

Grayscale Scanner

A grayscale scanner reads images using black, white and shades of gray. A grayscale scanner is ideal for scanning text or when you plan to print scanned images on a black-and-white printer.

Color Scanner

A color scanner is more expensive than a grayscale scanner and reads images using shades of red, blue and green. A color scanner is ideal for scanning images you plan to display in color, such as photographs and illustrations.

Choose the Scanning Mode

When scanning an image, you can choose the scanning mode.

Line Art

The line art mode scans an image using black and white.

Grayscale

The grayscale mode scans an image using black, white and shades of gray.

Color

The color mode scans an image using shades of red, blue and green.

RESOLUTION

The resolution of a scanner determines the amount of detail the scanner can detect.

Scanner resolution is measured in dots per inch (dpi). Some scanners can detect up to 2400 dpi.

Choose the Resolution

Scanning an image at a high resolution results in a clearer, more detailed image, but requires more scanning time and storage space.

You usually do not need to scan an image at a higher resolution than a printer can produce or a monitor can display.

20 dpi

72 dpi

300 dpi

If you plan to print an image on a 300 dpi printer, you do not need to scan at a resolution higher than 300 dpi. Monitors have a maximum resolution of 72 dpi. If you plan to display an image on a monitor or on the Internet, you do not need to scan at a resolution higher than 72 dpi.

DIGITAL CAMERA

A digital camera lets you take photos and use them on your computer.

You can place the photos in documents, on the World Wide Web or in e-mail messages to share them with your friends and relatives.

PROGRAMS

Most digital cameras come with a program called an image editor. Image editors allow you to view and edit photos on your computer. For example, you can change the colors or add and remove objects in your photos. Popular image editors include Adobe Systems PhotoDeluxe and Microsoft Picture It!

FEATURES

Most digital cameras come with a color Liquid Crystal Display (LCD) screen, which is the same type of display found in notebook computers. You can use the LCD screen to preview your shots and view photos you have taken.

A digital camera may also include a built-in flash or a zoom lens. Some digital cameras include a feature that lets you connect the camera to a TV so you can view your pictures on the screen.

RESOLUTION

The resolution of a digital camera determines the quality of photos the camera can produce.

The higher the resolution, the clearer and more detailed the photos. A digital camera with a resolution of 640 x 480 can produce photos suitable for viewing on a monitor. Digital cameras with a resolution of 1,152 x 864 or higher, called megapixel cameras, are best if you want to print good quality photos.

640 x 480

1,152 x 864

MEMORY

Digital cameras store photos in memory until you transfer the photos to your computer. Most digital cameras have either built-in or removable memory.

Built-in

The built-in memory in most digital cameras can store at least 20 photos. Once the built-in memory is full, you must transfer the photos to your computer before taking more photos.

Removable

Most digital cameras with removable memory store photos on a memory card. Some digital cameras store photos on a regular 3.5 inch floppy disk that fits inside the camera. You can replace a memory card or floppy disk when it is full.

PROCESSING

Memory, also called Random Access Memory (RAM), temporarily stores data inside a computer.

Memory works like a blackboard that is constantly overwritten with new data. The data stored in memory disappears when you turn off the computer.

MEMORY SIZE

The amount of memory determines the number of programs a computer can run at once and how fast programs will operate.

Memory is measured in bytes. You should buy a computer with at least 32 MB of memory, but 64 MB is recommended.

You can improve the performance of a computer by adding more memory.

PROGRAM REQUIREMENTS

A program will usually tell you the minimum amount of memory your computer needs to use the program.

System Requirements
- Pentium 90 MHz or higher
- Windows 95 or higher
- Memory: 16 MB
- Minimum install: 30 MB
- Monitor: VGA or above
- Mouse or other pointing device

WORD PROCESSOR V 5.0
Create Professional Documents

MEMORY CHIPS

Dynamic RAM (DRAM) is a type of memory chip that makes up the main memory in many computer systems.

Synchronous DRAM (SDRAM) is a faster type of memory chip found in most new computer systems. Many new computers can use both DRAM and SDRAM memory chips.

Memory Module

A memory module is a circuit board that holds memory chips. A Single In-line Memory Module (SIMM) holds up to nine memory chips. New computers also accept Dual In-line Memory Modules (DIMMs), which can hold up to 18 memory chips. You can add more memory to a computer by inserting additional memory modules.

Memory Module Socket

A memory module socket is a socket on the motherboard where you plug in a memory module.

VIRTUAL MEMORY

If you have limited memory or you have many programs open, your computer may need to use part of the hard drive to simulate more memory.

This simulated memory is called virtual memory and allows the computer to continue operating, but at a much slower speed.

ROM

Unlike RAM, Read-Only Memory (ROM) is permanent and cannot be changed. ROM stores instructions that help prepare the computer for use each time you turn on the computer.

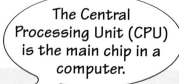

The Central Processing Unit (CPU) is the main chip in a computer.

The CPU processes instructions, performs calculations and manages the flow of information through a computer system. The CPU performs millions of calculations every second.

The CPU is also called the microprocessor or processor.

CPU COMPLEXITY

Imagine a U.S. road map printed on a fingernail and you can imagine the complexity of a CPU. The elements in a CPU can be as small as 0.18 microns wide. By comparison, a human hair is about 100 microns wide.

The manufacturing plants that produce CPUs are tens of thousands of times cleaner than hospital operating rooms. Ultra-sensitive dust filtering systems are needed to eliminate particles that could damage the CPUs.

CHOOSE A CPU

There are several factors that determine the performance of a CPU.

Manufacturer

The most popular CPUs for personal computers are made by Intel. Other companies that make CPUs include AMD and Cyrix.

Generation

Each new generation of CPUs is more powerful than the one before. Newer CPUs can process more instructions at a time.

CPU generations include the new Pentium II and the Pentium. The older 486 generation is obsolete.

When buying a new computer, do not consider anything less powerful than a Pentium II.

Speed

Each CPU generation is available in several speeds. The CPU speed is a major factor in determining how fast a computer operates. The faster the speed, the faster the computer operates.

The speed of a CPU is measured in megahertz (MHz), or millions of cycles per second.

TYPES OF CPUs

Pentium

Intel's Pentium chip is ideal for computers using Windows 3.1, 95 and 98. The most common speeds for Pentium chips include 90, 133, 166 and 200 MHz.

Comparable CPU chips include Cyrix's 6x86 and MediaGX chips, as well as AMD's AMD-K5 chip.

MMX

Many Pentium chips with speeds of 166 MHz and higher support multimedia extensions, referred to as MMX. MMX dramatically improves the performance of multimedia tasks, such as the processing of graphics, video and sound. Intel is working on a new version of MMX, currently named Katmai.

Pentium II

Intel's Pentium II chip is the fastest CPU chip available and is ideal for computers using Windows 98 and NT. All Pentium II chips support MMX technology for improved multimedia performance.

Pentium II chips are available with speeds of 233, 266, 300, 333, 350, 400, 450 and 500 MHz.

Comparable CPU chips include Cyrix's 6x86MX and M II chips, as well as AMD's AMD-K6 chip. These chips also support MMX technology.

Celeron

The Celeron chip is a fast and inexpensive CPU chip made by Intel. Celeron chips are based on Pentium II chips, but have less built-in memory. The Celeron chip is designed to meet the needs and budgets of most home computer users.

Celeron chips are available with speeds of 266, 300 and 333 MHz.

Pentium Pro

Intel's Pentium Pro chip is ideal for computers that use powerful operating systems, such as Windows NT and UNIX. Pentium Pro chips are available with speeds of 150, 166, 180 and 200 MHz.

The successor to the Pentium Pro chip is called the Pentium II Xeon.

Future CPUs

Intel's next generation of CPUs is expected to go well beyond the speed of the current Pentium II chips. This new CPU generation, currently named Merced, is being designed primarily for use in powerful network computers.

RAM (Main Memory)

Memory cache speeds up the computer by storing data the computer has recently used.

There are two types of memory cache—internal cache and external cache.

Internal Cache

External Cache

INTERNAL CACHE

When the computer needs data, the computer first looks in the internal cache. Internal cache is on the CPU chip and provides the fastest way for the computer to get data. Internal cache is also called L1 or primary cache.

EXTERNAL CACHE

If the computer cannot find the data it needs in the internal cache, the computer looks in the external cache. External cache is usually on the motherboard and consists of Static RAM (SRAM) chips.

Accessing external cache is generally slower than internal cache, but is much faster than retrieving data from RAM. In Pentium II and Pentium Pro chips, the external cache is built into the CPU chip, which makes accessing the cache much faster.

RAM

If the computer cannot find the data it needs in the internal or external cache, the computer must get the data from the slower main memory, called RAM.

Each time the computer requests data from RAM, the computer places a copy of the data in the memory cache. This process constantly updates the memory cache so it always contains the most recently used data.

USING MEMORY CACHE

Using memory cache is similar to working with documents in your office. When you need information, you look for information in a specific order. Each step along the way takes up more of your valuable time.

❶ Look through documents on your desk (internal cache).

❷ Look through documents in your desk drawer (external cache).

❸ Look through documents in your filing cabinet (RAM).

Working without memory cache would be similar to looking through the filing cabinet each time you need a document.

The bus is the electronic pathway in a computer that carries information between devices.

Bus Width

The bus width is similar to the number of lanes on a highway. The greater the width, the more data can flow along the bus at a time. Bus width is measured in bits. Eight bits equals one character.

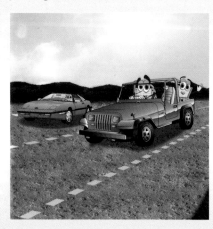

Bus Speed

The bus speed is similar to the speed limit on a highway. The higher the speed, the faster data travels along the bus. Bus speed is measured in megahertz (MHz), or millions of cycles per second.

ISA Bus

The Industry Standard Architecture (ISA) bus is the slowest and oldest type of bus. This bus is often used for transferring information to and from a slow device, such as a modem. The ISA bus has a width of 16 bits and a speed of 8 MHz.

The ISA bus is found in Pentium and Pentium II computers.

PCI Bus

The Peripheral Component Interconnect (PCI) bus is a sophisticated type of bus found in most new computers. This bus can handle many high-speed devices. The PCI bus can have a width of 32 or 64 bits and speeds of up to 100 MHz.

The PCI bus supports Plug and Play, which lets you add new devices to a computer without complex installation procedures.

The PCI bus is found in Pentium and Pentium II computers.

AGP Bus

An Accelerated Graphics Port (AGP) bus is specifically designed to carry complex graphics data between an AGP video card and your computer's main memory. The AGP bus has a width of 32 bits and a speed of 66 MHz.

The AGP bus is found in Pentium II computers.

STORAGE DEVICES

The hard drive is the primary device that a computer uses to store information.

■ Most computers have one hard drive, located inside the computer case. If a computer has one hard drive, it is called drive C. If a computer has additional hard drives, they are called drives D, E, F, and so on.

The hard drive is also called the hard disk, hard disk drive or fixed disk drive.

■ The hard drive light is on when the computer is using the hard drive. Do not move the computer when this light is on.

Inside a Hard Drive

The hard drive magnetically stores data on a stack of rotating disks, called platters.

■ A hard drive has several read/write heads that read and record data on the disks.

HARD DRIVE CONTENTS

Program Files

A hard drive stores your programs. When you buy a new program, you must install, or copy, the program files to your hard drive before you can use the program.

Programs come on a CD-ROM disc, DVD-ROM disc or several floppy disks.

Data Files

A hard drive stores your data files such as documents, spreadsheets and graphics.

STORE FILES

Save Files

When you are creating a document, the computer stores the document in temporary memory. If you want to store a document for future use, you must save the document to the hard drive. If you do not save the document, the document will be lost when there is a power failure or you turn off the computer.

Organize Files

Like a filing cabinet, a hard drive uses folders or directories to organize information.

CHOOSE A HARD DRIVE

Capacity

The amount of information a hard drive can store is measured in bytes.

A hard drive with a capacity of 3 to 4 GB will suit most home and business users.

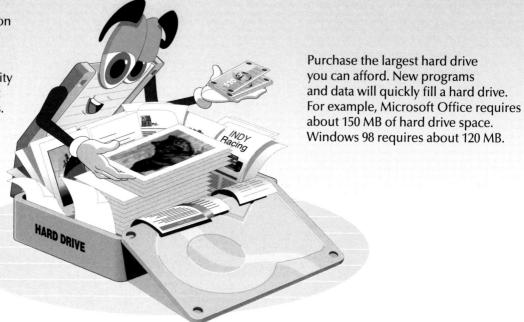

Purchase the largest hard drive you can afford. New programs and data will quickly fill a hard drive. For example, Microsoft Office requires about 150 MB of hard drive space. Windows 98 requires about 120 MB.

Speed

The speed at which the rotating disks in the hard drive, called platters, spin is measured in Revolutions Per Minute (RPM). The higher the RPM, the faster the hard drive can find and record data on the platters.

The speed at which a hard drive finds data is referred to as the average access time. Average access time is measured in milliseconds (ms). One millisecond equals 1/1000 of a second. Most hard drives have an average access time of 8 to 15 ms. The lower the average access time, the faster the hard drive.

CONNECTION TYPE

EIDE

Enhanced Integrated Drive Electronics (EIDE) is a fast way to connect a hard drive and other devices to a computer. All new computers come with an EIDE connection. EIDE is often referred to as IDE.

EIDE can support a total of four devices, including hard drives, CD-ROM drives, DVD-ROM drives and tape drives.

Ultra Direct Memory Access (UDMA) is an enhancement to EIDE that increases the speed at which data transfers over an EIDE connection.

SCSI

Small Computer System Interface (SCSI) is the fastest, most flexible, but most expensive way to connect a hard drive and other devices to a computer. SCSI is pronounced "scuzzy."

The most common type of SCSI can connect up to seven devices, including removable drives, CD-ROM drives, DVD-ROM drives, tape drives and scanners. There are also other types of SCSI available that transmit data faster and connect more devices.

DISK CACHE

The disk cache speeds up the computer by storing data the computer has recently used.

■ The disk cache is an area of memory where the computer stores recently used data.

When the computer needs data, the computer first looks in the disk cache. The disk cache can supply data thousands of times faster than the hard drive.

If the computer cannot find the data it needs in the disk cache, the computer looks on the hard drive.

Each time the computer requests data from the hard drive, the computer places a copy of the data in the disk cache. This process constantly updates the disk cache so it always contains the most recently used data.

HARD DRIVE

DISK CACHE

PROTECT A HARD DRIVE

Virus

A virus is a program that disrupts the normal operation of a computer. A virus can cause a variety of problems, such as the appearance of annoying messages on the screen or the destruction of information on the hard drive.

Files you receive on a floppy disk or from the Internet may contain viruses. You should regularly use an anti-virus program to check for viruses on your computer.

Back Up Data

You should copy the files stored on your hard drive to removable disks or tape cartridges. This provides extra copies in case the original files are stolen or damaged due to viruses or computer failure.

You only need to back up your own work. You do not need to back up programs stored on your computer since you can use the original program disks to re-install the programs.

OPTIMIZE A HARD DRIVE

Defragment a Drive

A fragmented hard drive stores parts of a file in many different locations. To retrieve a file, the computer must search many areas of the drive.

You can use a defragmentation program to place all parts of a file in one location. This reduces the time the hard drive spends locating the file.

Defragmenting your hard drive once a month can improve the performance of the computer.

Windows 95 and 98 include a defragmentation program.

Repair a Drive

You can improve the performance of a computer by using a disk repair program to search for and repair disk errors. You should check a hard drive for errors at least once a month.

Windows 95 and 98 include a disk repair program.

CREATE MORE DISK SPACE

Archive Information

Store old or rarely used files on a tape cartridge or a removable disk. You can then remove the files from your computer to provide more storage space.

FAT32

You may be able to convert your hard drive to the FAT32 file system to better manage data on the drive and reduce wasted space. For example, converting a 1 GB drive to FAT32 may increase the amount of free space on the drive by over 200 MB.

Windows 98 includes a program you can use to convert your drive to FAT32.

Data Compression

You can compress, or squeeze together, the files stored on a hard drive. This can double the amount of information the drive can store.

You should only compress a hard drive if it is running out of space to store new information and you have tried all other ways of increasing the available storage space.

Windows 95 and 98 include a disk compression program.

A floppy drive stores and retrieves information on floppy disks.

All computers have a floppy drive, called drive A.

FLOPPY DISK

A floppy drive stores information on floppy disks, or diskettes. A floppy disk is a removable device that magnetically stores data.

Floppy disks are commonly used for transferring data from one computer to another. This lets you give data to friends and colleagues.

Floppy drives use 3.5 inch floppy disks. Inside a 3.5 inch floppy disk is a thin, plastic, flexible disk that magnetically records information. The word floppy refers to this flexible disk.

INSERT A FLOPPY DISK

Push the floppy disk gently into the drive, label side up. Most drives make a "click" sound when you have fully inserted the disk.

■ This light is on when the computer is using the floppy disk. Do not remove the disk when this light is on.

■ To remove the floppy disk, press this button.

PROTECT A FLOPPY DISK

You can prevent erasing and recording information on a floppy disk by sliding the tab to the write-protected position.

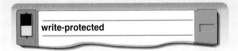

write-protected

You **cannot** erase and record information.

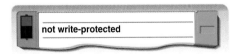

not write-protected

You **can** erase and record information.

Make sure you keep floppy disks away from magnets, which can damage the information stored on the disks. Also make sure you do not store floppy disks in extremely hot or cold locations and try not to spill liquids such as coffee or soda on the disks.

A CD-ROM drive is a device that reads information stored on compact discs.

Most CD-ROM drives are located inside the computer case. External CD-ROM drives that connect to the computer by a cable are also available.

CD-ROM DISC

A CD-ROM disc is the same type of disc you buy at a music store.

A single CD-ROM disc can store more than 600 MB of data. This is equal to an entire set of encyclopedias or over 400 floppy disks. The large storage capacity of CD-ROM discs leaves more room for storing large images, animation and video.

CD-ROM stands for Compact Disc-Read-Only Memory. Read-only means you cannot change the information stored on a disc.

CD-ROM APPLICATIONS

Install Programs

The large storage capacity of a CD-ROM disc makes installing new programs on your computer easy. A program that requires 20 floppy disks can easily fit on a single CD-ROM disc.

Play Multimedia CD-ROM Discs

A CD-ROM disc can store multimedia presentations. Multimedia refers to the combination of text, graphics, sound, animation and video. Multimedia provides a powerful way of communicating information.

There are thousands of multimedia CD-ROM discs available to inform and entertain you. You can buy multimedia CD-ROM discs at most computer stores.

Play Music CDs

You can play music CDs on a CD-ROM drive while you work.

CD-ROM DRIVE SPEED

The speed of a CD-ROM drive determines how fast a disc spins. With faster speeds, information can transfer from a disc to the computer more quickly, which results in better performance.

Speed is very important when viewing video and animation often found in games and encyclopedias. Slow speeds will result in jerky performances.

The speed of a CD-ROM drive is called the data transfer rate or throughput and is measured in Kilobytes per second (KB/s).

CD-ROM DRIVE SPEED	MAXIMUM DATA TRANSFER RATE
Eight (8X)	1,200 KB/s
Ten (10X)	1,600 KB/s
Twelve (12X)	1,800 KB/s
Sixteen (16X)	2,400 KB/s
Twenty-Four (24X)	3,600 KB/s
Thirty-Two (32X)	4,800 KB/s

The chart to the left displays the most common speeds available. You should buy at least a 24X CD-ROM drive.

WORK WITH A CD-ROM DISC

Insert a Disc

■ To insert or remove a disc, press this button.

■ A tray slides out. Place the disc, label side up, on the tray. To close the tray, press the button again.

■ This light is on when the CD-ROM drive is accessing information on the disc.

Headphones

You can use headphones to listen to recorded sounds on a disc. Headphones are useful in noisy environments or when you want to listen to a disc privately.

Handle a Disc

When handling a CD-ROM disc, hold the disc around the edges.

Protect a Disc

When you finish using a disc, make sure you place the disc back in its protective case. Do not stack discs on top of each other.

CD-ROM DRIVE

CD-R DRIVE

> A CD-R (Compact Disc-Recordable) drive is a device that allows you to permanently store information on a compact disc.

A CD-R drive can also play CD-ROM discs and music CDs.

CD-R DRIVE APPLICATIONS

Store and Transfer Data

You can use a CD-R drive to store up to 650 MB of data on a single disc. This lets you easily transfer data, such as software applications or multimedia presentations, between computers.

CD-R discs are not erasable, so any data recorded onto a disc is permanent and cannot be changed.

Record Audio

A CD-R drive lets you create audio CDs that you can play on a CD-ROM drive or on a regular CD player. To record sound from a music CD or cassette onto a CD-R disc, you can attach your stereo system to your computer. A single CD-R disc can store up to 74 minutes of audio.

CD-R SOFTWARE

A CD-R drive requires special software to record data onto a CD-R disc. Many CD-R drives come with software specifically designed for use with the drive. You can also purchase software that provides more features, such as utilities to improve the quality of the sound you are recording.

CD-R DRIVE SPEED

Write Speed

Read Speed

A CD-R drive operates at two different speeds. The write speed refers to how fast the drive can record data onto a disc. Common CD-R write speeds include 2X and 4X. The read speed refers to how fast data transfers from a disc to the computer. Common CD-R read speeds include 6X, 8X and 12X.

CD-RW DRIVE

A CD-RW (Compact Disc-ReWritable) drive is similar to a CD-R drive, but allows you to change the data you record on a disc many times. A CD-RW disc stores the same amount of data as a CD-R disc.

Discs created on CD-RW drives may not work in some CD-R and CD-ROM drives, or in some CD players.

A DVD-ROM drive is a device that reads information stored on DVD-ROM or CD-ROM discs.

DVD-ROM stands for Digital Versatile Disc-Read-Only Memory. Read-only means you cannot change the information stored on a disc.

A DVD-ROM disc is similar in size and shape to a CD-ROM disc, but can store a lot more information.

DVD-ROM APPLICATIONS

Multimedia

You can use a DVD-ROM drive to play multimedia DVD-ROM discs, CD-ROM discs and music CDs. Some DVD-ROM drives, called second generation drives, can also play CDs recorded on CD-R and CD-RW drives.

DVD-Video

DVD-ROM drives can play DVD-Video discs, which hold full-length, full-screen movies with much better quality than VHS tapes. Many DVD-Video discs allow you to change the way you view the movie, such as displaying subtitles.

Special hardware, such as an MPEG-2 video decoder card, may be required for the best playback of DVD-Video.

DVD CONSIDERATIONS

DVD Disc Storage Capacity

A single DVD disc can store at least 4.7 GB of data, which equals over seven CD-ROM discs.

DVD DISC	1 side/ 1 layer	1 side/ 2 layers	2 sides/ 1 layer	2 sides/ 2 layers
Storage	4.7 GB	8.5 GB	9.4 GB	17 GB

Unlike CD-ROM discs, DVD discs can be single-sided or double-sided. Each side can store one or two layers of data.

DVD-ROM Drive Speed

The speed of a DVD-ROM drive determines how quickly data can transfer from a disc to the computer. Many DVD-ROM drives, called 1X drives, have a speed equivalent to an 8X CD-ROM drive. Newer DVD-ROM drives, called 2X drives, can reach speeds equivalent to a 24X CD-ROM drive.

RECORDABLE DVD DRIVE

Recordable DVD drives allow you to record data on DVD discs. Most recordable DVD drives are rewritable, which means you can change the data recorded on the disc. Most recordable DVD drives can also play DVD, CD-ROM, CD-R and CD-RW discs, as well as music CDs.

A tape drive is a device that copies files from a computer onto tape cartridges.

Tape drives are also called tape backup units.

A tape drive can be inside the computer case or connected to the computer by a cable. An external tape drive is more expensive, but can be used with more than one computer.

Tape Cartridges

A tape drive stores information on tape cartridges. These cartridges are similar to the cassettes you buy at music stores.

Store all cartridges in a cool, dry place, away from electrical equipment.

TAPE DRIVE APPLICATIONS

Back Up Data

Most people use tape drives to make backup copies of files stored on a computer. This provides extra copies in case the original files are stolen or damaged due to viruses or computer failure. Most people should back up their work every day.

Archive Data

You can copy old or rarely used files from your computer to tape cartridges. You can then remove the files from your computer to provide more storage space.

Transfer Data

You can use a tape drive to transfer large amounts of information between computers. Make sure the person receiving the information uses the same type of tape drive.

BACKUP PROGRAM

A backup program helps you copy the files stored on your computer to tape cartridges.

Most tape drives come with a backup program specifically designed for use with the tape drive. Windows 95 and 98 also include a backup program.

Schedule Backups

You can set a backup program to run automatically. This lets you schedule a backup at night, when you are not using your computer.

Full   **Incremental**

Types of Backups

A full backup will back up all your files. An incremental backup will back up only the files that have changed since the last backup. An incremental backup saves you time when backing up a lot of information.

Compress Data

A backup program can compress, or squeeze together, data you are backing up. This may allow you to double the amount of data you can store on a tape cartridge.

CHOOSE A TAPE DRIVE

When buying a tape drive, you should choose a drive that can store the entire contents of your hard drive on a single tape cartridge. This will make it easier to perform a full backup of your hard drive.

Travan Drive

Travan drives are the most common type of tape drive. There are several levels of Travan drives and tape cartridges, including TR-1, TR-2, TR-3 and TR-4. The higher the level, the more data the drive or tape cartridge can store. Travan drives can accept different levels of tape cartridges. A high-quality Travan drive can store up to 10 GB of data on a single Travan cartridge.

DAT Drive

A Digital Audio Tape (DAT) drive is faster than a Travan drive, but is more expensive. A high-quality DAT drive can store up to 24 GB of data on a single DAT cartridge.

TAPE CARTRIDGES TIP

Companies often advertise the amount of compressed data a tape cartridge can store. Companies assume that compression will double the amount of information a cartridge can store. This is not always the case.

The amount of information that is actually compressed depends on the type of information you are storing. For example, a text file will compress significantly more than a graphics file.

REMOVABLE DRIVE

A removable drive is a storage device that allows you to store large amounts of data on removable disks.

Removable disks are similar in size and shape to floppy disks.

REMOVABLE DRIVE APPLICATIONS

Archive Data

You can use a removable drive to store old or rarely used files. You can then remove the files from your computer to provide more storage space.

Protect Data

You can use a removable drive to store confidential data or backup copies of data. You can then protect the data by placing the disks in a safe place on nights and weekends.

Transfer Data

You can use a removable drive to transfer large amounts of data between computers. For example, you can take work home or transfer data to a colleague.

When using a removable drive to transfer data, you must ensure that the person receiving the data uses the same type of drive. Most removable drives cannot use disks from a different type of drive.

TYPES OF REMOVABLE DRIVES

There are several popular types of removable drives. Many new computers now come with built-in removable drives.

Jaz® Drive

Jaz® drives are currently one of the most popular types of removable drives. Jaz® drives are very fast and have the largest storage capacity of all removable drives. Some Jaz® drives can store up to 2 GB of data on a single disk.

SyJet Drive

A SyJet drive is a very fast removable drive. A SyJet drive can store up to 1.5 GB of data on a single cartridge.

Zip® Drive

Zip® drives are currently a very popular type of removable drive. A Zip® drive is relatively inexpensive and can store up to 100 MB of data on a single disk.

SuperDisk Drive

A SuperDisk drive can store up to 120 MB of data on a single disk. Unlike many other removable drives, SuperDisk drives also accept regular 3.5 inch floppy disks.

PORTABLE COMPUTERS

A notebook is a small, lightweight computer that you can easily transport.

A notebook computer is also called a laptop.

You can buy a notebook computer with the same capabilities as a desktop computer, although notebook computers are more expensive.

A notebook computer has a built-in keyboard, pointing device and screen. This eliminates the need for cables to connect these devices to the notebook.

ADVANTAGES OF NOTEBOOKS

Travel

A notebook computer lets you work when traveling or outdoors. You can also use a notebook computer to bring work home instead of staying late at the office.

Presentations

You can bring a notebook computer to meetings to present information.

BATTERY

A battery or an electrical outlet can supply the power for a notebook computer.

A battery lets you use a notebook when no electrical outlets are available.

TYPES OF BATTERIES

There are two main types of batteries—nickel metal hydride (NiMH) and lithium-ion. Lithium-ion is a more expensive battery, but is lighter and lasts longer than NiMH. Some notebook computers now use Smart batteries. Smart batteries help notebooks better manage power consumption.

MONITOR A BATTERY

Most notebooks display the amount of battery power remaining, either on the screen or on a panel built into the computer.

RECHARGE A BATTERY

The power supplied by most batteries lasts for only a few hours. You must recharge a battery before you can use it again. If you are unable to recharge a battery when traveling, bring an extra battery so you can work for a longer period of time.

SCREEN

The screen on a notebook computer uses Liquid Crystal Display (LCD). This is the same type of display found in most digital wristwatches.

An LCD screen uses very little power, which extends the length of time you can use a battery before needing to recharge. An LCD screen also weighs much less than a desktop monitor, which makes a notebook easier to carry.

BACKLIGHT

Notebooks have an internal light source that illuminates the back of the screen. This makes the screen easier to view in poorly lit areas but shortens the length of time you can use a battery before needing to recharge.

POWER A FULL-SIZE MONITOR

Most notebooks can use both the notebook screen and a full-size monitor at the same time. This feature is very useful when delivering presentations.

SCREEN SIZE

The size of the screen is measured diagonally. Screen sizes range from about 12 to 15 inches.

TYPES OF SCREENS

Passive Matrix

This type of screen is less expensive than an active matrix screen, but is not as bright or rich in color. The lower cost makes a passive matrix screen ideal for routine office tasks.

A passive matrix screen is also called a Double SuperTwisted Nematic (DSTN) screen.

Passive matrix screens can be difficult to read when viewed from an angle. This is ideal when you want to keep work private from people sitting next to you on a train or plane, but makes delivering a presentation to several people difficult.

Active Matrix

This type of screen is more expensive, but displays brighter, richer colors than a passive matrix screen.

An active matrix screen is also called a Thin-Film Transistor (TFT) screen.

You can view an active matrix screen from wide angles, which makes it more suitable for delivering presentations to several people.

INPUT AND OUTPUT DEVICES

There are several devices that let you move the pointer around the screen of a notebook computer.

A mouse is impractical when traveling, since you need a relatively large, flat surface to move the mouse.

Pointing Stick

A pointing stick is a small, eraser-like device that you push in different directions to move the pointer on the screen.

Trackball

A trackball is an upside-down mouse that remains stationary. You roll the ball with your fingers or palm to move the pointer on the screen. Built-in trackballs on the right side of the keyboard may be awkward for left-handed users.

Touchpad

A touchpad is a surface that is sensitive to pressure and motion. When you move your fingertip across the pad, the pointer on the screen moves in the same direction.

KEYBOARD

The keys on a notebook keyboard may be small and close together to save space. Before buying a notebook, type several paragraphs of text to make sure the keyboard is suitable for you.

Some notebook computers have a keyboard that expands to a full-size keyboard.

MODEM

You can buy a notebook with a built-in modem or add modem capabilities later.

A modem allows you to connect to the Internet to exchange information and messages.

When traveling, a modem also lets you connect to the network at work.

SOUND CARD AND SPEAKERS

You can buy a notebook with a built-in sound card and speakers to play and record sound. This is very useful when you want to use the notebook to deliver presentations.

STORAGE DEVICES

HARD DRIVE

The hard drive is the primary device a notebook uses to store information. Buy the largest hard drive you can afford. New programs and data will quickly fill a hard drive.

CD-ROM OR DVD-ROM DRIVE

A notebook computer can include a CD-ROM drive or a DVD-ROM drive to read information stored on Compact Discs (CDs) or Digital Versatile Discs (DVDs).

Some notebooks let you remove the CD-ROM or DVD-ROM drive and replace it with another component. This new component could be an extra battery to increase the amount of time you can use the notebook, a second hard drive for additional storage space or a floppy drive.

FLOPPY DRIVE

Many notebooks come with a floppy drive to store and retrieve information on floppy disks.

If you will not use a floppy drive very often, you can buy a notebook without a floppy drive to reduce the notebook's weight. You can then connect the notebook to an external floppy drive when necessary.

PROCESSING

CPU

The Central Processing Unit (CPU) is the main chip in a computer. The CPU processes instructions, performs calculations and manages the flow of information through a computer system.

The most popular CPUs for notebook computers are made by Intel. Other companies that make CPUs for notebooks include AMD and Cyrix.

This chart shows the most common CPU chips available for notebook computers. Which chip you decide to buy depends on your budget and how you plan to use the computer.

CPU	SPEED (MHz)
Pentium with MMX	150 166 200 233
Pentium II	233 266

MEMORY

Electronic memory, or RAM, temporarily stores data inside a computer. Memory works like a blackboard that is constantly overwritten with new data. A notebook computer running Windows 98 should have at least 32 MB of memory to ensure that programs run smoothly.

PC CARD

A PC Card adds a new capability, such as sound or additional memory, to a notebook computer.

Some PC Cards provide multiple features. For example, a single PC Card can provide networking and modem capabilities.

A PC Card used to be called a PCMCIA Card. PCMCIA stands for Personal Computer Memory Card International Association.

TYPES OF PC CARDS

A PC Card is a lightweight device about the size of a credit card. There are three types of PC Cards—Type I, Type II and Type III. Type I is the thinnest card, while Type III is the thickest. Each type of card can vary in the features it offers.

Some notebooks support a new type of PC Card, called a CardBus card. These cards enhance a notebook's ability to perform demanding tasks, such as videoconferencing.

PC SLOT

You insert a PC Card into a slot on a notebook computer. Most notebook computers have a PC slot that can accept both a Type I and Type II PC Card or one Type III PC Card.

USE A NOTEBOOK AT WORK

Network Interface Card

A network interface card connects a notebook to a network and controls the flow of information between the network and the notebook. When connected to a network, you can access all the equipment and information available on the network.

Infrared Port

Some notebook computers have an infrared port to share information without using cables. Infrared ports are commonly used for connecting a notebook computer to a printer.

Port Replicator

A port replicator lets you connect many devices, such as a printer, modem and mouse, to a notebook at once. After you connect a notebook to a port replicator, you can use all the devices attached to the port replicator without having to attach each device to the notebook individually.

Docking Station

A docking station lets you connect many devices to a notebook at once. A docking station can also provide additional features, such as networking capabilities and a full-size monitor and keyboard.

A handheld computer is a portable computer small enough to carry in your hand.

A handheld computer is also called a Personal Digital Assistant (PDA) or pocket computer.

Handheld computers are capable of storing thousands of addresses, appointments and memos. You can use a handheld computer to exchange electronic mail, send and receive faxes and browse the World Wide Web. Some handheld computers also come with word processing and spreadsheet applications.

You can connect a handheld computer to a desktop computer to exchange data between the two computers.

INPUT DEVICES

Keyboard

Handheld computers have a small keyboard that allows you to input data.

Stylus

Instead of a mouse, handheld computers use an electronic pen, called a stylus, to select objects on the screen.

Modem

You can buy a handheld computer with a built-in modem or you can add modem capabilities later. A modem allows you to connect to the Internet.

OPERATING SYSTEMS

Most handheld computers use the Microsoft Windows CE operating system to control the overall activity of the computer. Windows CE is a Graphical User Interface (GUI, pronounced "gooey"). A GUI allows you to use pictures instead of text commands to perform tasks. The latest version of Windows CE comes with limited versions of popular Microsoft Office applications.

PALM COMPUTERS

Palm computers are small handheld computers that are often used as electronic organizers. You can connect a palm computer to a desktop computer to exchange data between the two computers.

Palm computers have many of the same features as handheld computers, but they do not have a keyboard. You use a stylus, or electronic pen, to input data into a palm computer.

Like handheld computers, palm computers also use an operating system to control the overall activity of the computer. Some palm computers use the Windows CE operating system, but there are other operating systems available.

Popular palm computers include 3COM's PalmPilot and Palm III.

APPLICATION SOFTWARE

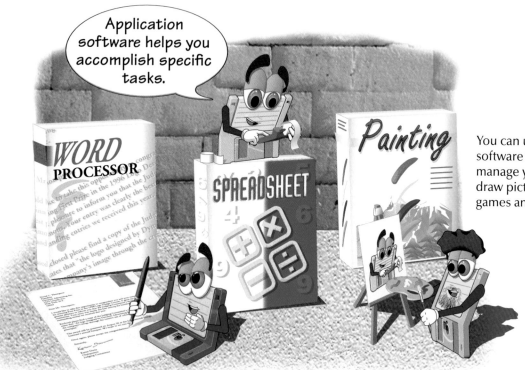

Application software helps you accomplish specific tasks.

You can use application software to write letters, manage your finances, draw pictures, play games and much more.

Application software is also called software, an application or a program.

GET SOFTWARE

You can buy software at computer stores. There are also thousands of programs available on the Internet.

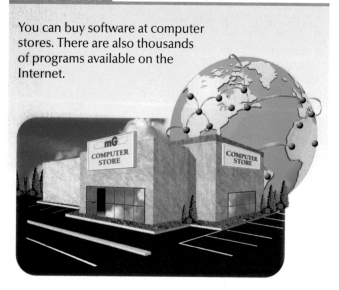

INSTALL SOFTWARE

Software you buy at a computer store may come on a CD-ROM disc, a DVD-ROM disc or several floppy disks. Before you can use the software, you must install, or copy, the contents of the disc or disks to your computer. Using a CD-ROM or DVD-ROM disc is a fast method of installing software.

SOFTWARE VERSION

Software developers and manufacturers constantly make corrections (called bug-fixes) and add new features to the software they create. When a manufacturer releases updated software, the software is given a new version number. This helps people distinguish new versions of the software from older versions.

BUNDLED SOFTWARE

Bundled software is software that comes with a new computer system or device, such as a printer. Companies often include bundled software to let you start using the new equipment right away. For example, new computer systems usually come with word processing, spreadsheet and graphics programs.

GET HELP

Most software comes with a built-in help feature and printed documentation to help you learn to use the software. You can also buy computer books with detailed, step-by-step instructions at computer or book stores.

WORD PROCESSOR

A word processor helps you create professional-looking documents quickly and efficiently.

Popular word processing programs include Microsoft Word, Corel WordPerfect and Lotus Word Pro.

WORD PROCESSING HIGHLIGHTS

Documents

You can create many different types of documents, such as letters, reports, manuals, newsletters and brochures.

Editing

Word processors offer many features that help you work with text in documents. You can easily edit text, rearrange paragraphs and check for spelling mistakes.

Formatting

You can easily change the appearance of your documents. You can add page numbers, center text and use various fonts in a document.

Printing

You can produce a paper copy of a document. Word processors let you see on the screen exactly what a printed document will look like.

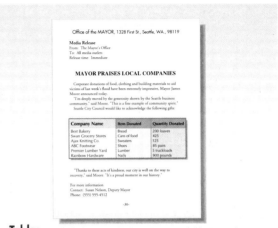

Tables

You can create tables to neatly organize information in a document. You can also add colors and borders to enhance the appearance of tables.

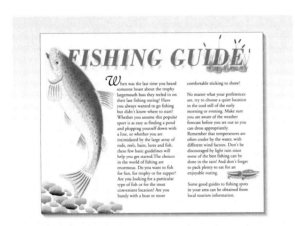

Graphics

Most word processors include many types of graphics that you can use to enhance the appearance of your documents.

Mail Merge

Word processors offer a merge feature that lets you quickly produce personalized letters, envelopes and mailing labels for each person on a mailing list.

SPREADSHEET

A spreadsheet program helps you manage personal and business finances.

PAYROLL 1997

PAYROLL 1996

ROLL 1995

Popular spreadsheet programs include Microsoft Excel and Lotus 1-2-3.

SPREADSHEET APPLICATIONS

Manage Finances

You can use a spreadsheet program to perform calculations, analyze data and present information.

Manage Data in a List

A spreadsheet program lets you store a large collection of information such as a mailing or product list. Spreadsheet programs include tools for organizing, managing, sorting and retrieving data.

If you want greater control over a list stored on your computer, use a database program. Database programs are specifically designed to manage a list of data.

SPREADSHEET FEATURES

Editing

When working with a spreadsheet program, you can add, delete, move or copy data. Most spreadsheet programs can remember the last change you made and let you undo, or cancel, the change.

Formatting

A spreadsheet program offers many features that help you enhance the appearance of your spreadsheets. You can easily change the design and size of data. You can also add color and borders to the cells in a spreadsheet.

Formulas and Functions

Spreadsheets provide powerful formulas and functions to calculate and analyze your data. A function is a ready-to-use formula that helps you perform specialized calculations.

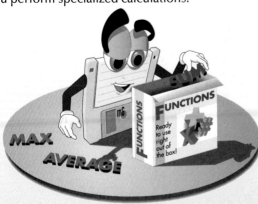

Charts

A chart lets you graphically display the data in a spreadsheet. After creating a chart, you can select a new type of chart that will better suit the data.

DATABASE

> A database program helps you manage large collections of information.

Database programs are commonly used to manage mailing lists, phone directories, product listings and payroll information.

Popular database programs include Microsoft Access and Lotus Approach.

PARTS OF A DATABASE

Table

A table is a collection of information about a specific topic, such as a mailing list. You can have one or more tables in a database.

Address ID	First Name	Last Name	Address	City	State/Province	Postal Code
1	Jim	Schmith	258 Linton Ave.	New York	NY	10010
2	Brenda	Petterson	50 Tree Lane	Boston	MA	02117
3	Todd	Talbot	68 Cracker Ave.	San Francisco	CA	94110
4	Chuck	Dean	47 Crosby Ave.	Las Vegas	NV	89116
5	Melanie	Robinson	26 Arnold Cres.	Jacksonville	FL	32256
6	Susan	Hughes	401 Idon Dr.	Nashville	TN	37243
7	Allen	Toppins	10 Heldon St.	Atlanta	GA	30375
8	Greg	Kilkenny	36 Buzzard St.	Boston	MA	02118
9	Jason	Marcuson	15 Bizzo Pl.	New York	NY	10020
10	Jim	Martin	890 Apple St.	San Diego	CA	92121

A table consists of fields and records.

Field

A field is a specific category of information in a table. For example, a field can contain the first names of all your clients.

Record

A record is a collection of information about one person, place or thing in a table. For example, a record can contain the name and address of one client.

DATABASE APPLICATIONS

Store Information

A database stores and manages a collection of information related to a particular subject or purpose.

You can easily add, update, view and organize the information stored in a database.

Find Information

You can instantly locate information of interest in a database. For example, you can find all clients with the last name Smith.

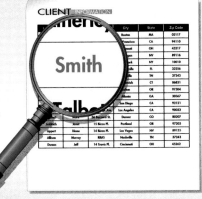

You can also perform more advanced searches, such as finding all clients who live in California and who purchased more than $100 of supplies last year.

Analyze and Print Information

You can perform calculations on the information in a database to help you make quick, accurate and informed decisions.

You can neatly present the information in professionally designed reports.

An application suite is a collection of programs sold together in one package.

ADVANTAGES

Cost

Buying programs as part of an application suite costs less than buying each program individually.

Easy to Use

Programs in an application suite share a common design and work in a similar way. Once you learn one program, you can easily learn the others.

DISADVANTAGE

Since all the programs in an application suite come from the same manufacturer, you may not get the best combination of features for your needs. Make sure you evaluate all the programs in an application suite before making your purchase.

APPLICATION SUITE PROGRAMS

Most application suites include four types of programs. Some application suites also offer additional programs, such as a scheduling program that lets you keep track of appointments.

Word Processing Program

A word processing program lets you create documents, such as letters and reports.

Spreadsheet Program

A spreadsheet program lets you manage and analyze financial information.

Presentation Program

A presentation program lets you design presentations.

Database Program

A database program lets you manage large collections of information. The database program may only be included in higher-priced versions of the suite.

POPULAR APPLICATION SUITES

Microsoft Office is the most popular application suite.

Other application suites include Corel WordPerfect Suite and Lotus SmartSuite.

You can buy many utility programs at computer stores. Some utility programs are also available for free on the Internet.

The utilities you can use depend on the operating system running on your computer.

Norton Utilities

Symantec's Norton Utilities provides tools to help you maintain and optimize your computer. Norton Utilities also includes tools to help you recover lost files and protect against computer failure.

VirusScan Security Suite

McAfee's VirusScan Security Suite is a collection of anti-virus programs you can use to reduce the risk of a virus infecting your computer. A virus is a program that can cause problems ranging from displaying annoying messages on your screen to erasing the information on your hard drive.

Acrobat Reader

Adobe Acrobat Reader is a program that allows you to view Portable Document Format (.pdf) files. These files are often used on the World Wide Web to display books and magazines exactly as they appear in printed form.

ViaVoice Gold

IBM's ViaVoice Gold is a speech recognition program that allows you to control your computer with your voice. You can speak to your computer to open files or dictate documents into a word processor.

WinFax Pro

With Symantec WinFax Pro, you can use your computer's fax modem to send and receive faxes. WinFax Pro can also convert the faxes you receive into documents that you can edit using a word processor.

WinZip

Nico Mak's WinZip helps you decompress files. Many of the files on the Internet are compressed, or squeezed together, and must be decompressed before you can use them on your computer.

WinZip also compresses information so files can transfer faster between computers.

GAME SOFTWARE

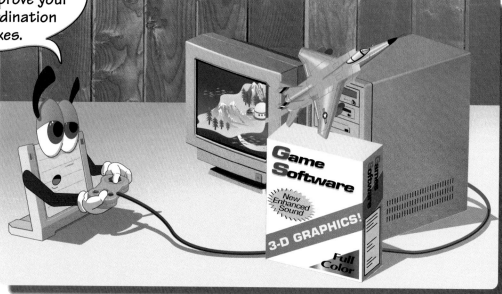

You can play games on your computer. This is a fun way to improve your hand-eye coordination and reflexes.

GAME HARDWARE

Game Controller

A game controller is a device, such as a joystick or gamepad, which allows you to interact with a game. Popular game controllers include Microsoft SideWinder and Gravis GamePad.

Some games require a specific type of game controller. Before buying a game, check to see what type of controller the game requires.

3D Graphics Card

Many games are designed with 3D graphics and run best on a computer with a 3D graphics card. A 3D graphics card is a circuit board that translates complex instructions from the computer into a form the monitor can understand. Popular 3D graphics cards include Matrox Millenium and Diamond Monster 3D.

Some games require a specific type of 3D graphics card. Before buying a game, check to see what type of card the game requires.

GAME CONSIDERATIONS

Types of Games

There are many different types of games available, including action, sports, strategy, simulation, puzzle and educational games. Games are available for all ages and skill levels.

Internet and Network Games

Many games are designed to let several people compete against each other on the Internet or on a network.

There are many online gaming services available that allow you to easily connect to other people on the Internet to play a game. When you play a game with other people on the Internet, each person usually has to have their own copy of the game.

Purchase Games

You can buy games at computer stores. There are also many games available on the Internet. Games can be very expensive, but game manufacturers often offer a trial version of their games for free on the World Wide Web, so you can try a game before you buy it.

OPERATING SYSTEMS

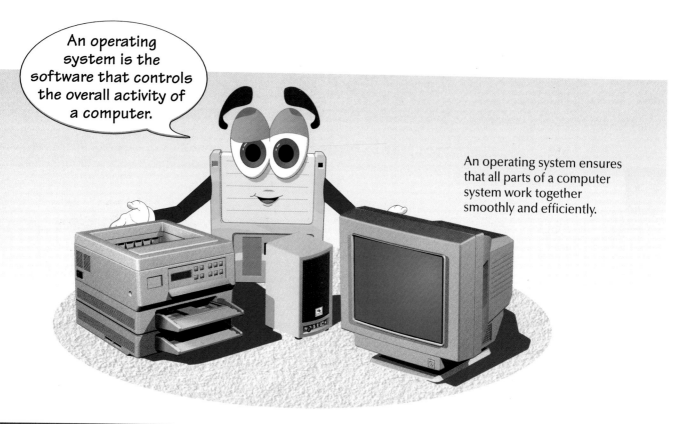

An operating system is the software that controls the overall activity of a computer.

An operating system ensures that all parts of a computer system work together smoothly and efficiently.

OPERATING SYSTEM FUNCTIONS

Control Hardware

An operating system controls the different parts of a computer system and enables all the parts to work together.

Run Application Software

An operating system runs application software, such as Microsoft Word and Lotus 1-2-3.

Manage Information

An operating system provides ways to manage and organize information stored on a computer. You can use an operating system to sort, copy, move, delete or view files.

TYPES OF OPERATING SYSTEMS

MS-DOS

MS-DOS stands for Microsoft Disk Operating System. MS-DOS displays lines of text on the screen. You perform tasks by typing short commands.

Windows

Windows displays a graphical screen. You use a mouse to perform tasks.

Windows is a Graphical User Interface (GUI, pronounced "gooey"). A GUI allows you to use pictures instead of text commands to perform tasks. This makes Windows easier to use than MS-DOS.

UNIX

UNIX is a powerful operating system used by many computers on the Internet. There are many different versions of the UNIX operating system available.

PLATFORM

A platform refers to the type of operating system used by a computer, such as MS-DOS or Windows. Programs used on one platform will not usually work on another platform.

For example, you cannot use Word for Windows on a computer running only MS-DOS.

MS-DOS is an operating system that performs tasks using text commands you enter.

MS-DOS stands for Microsoft Disk Operating System.

ENTER A COMMAND

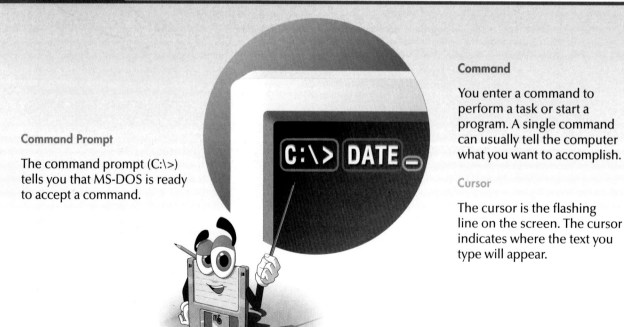

Command Prompt

The command prompt (C:\>) tells you that MS-DOS is ready to accept a command.

Command

You enter a command to perform a task or start a program. A single command can usually tell the computer what you want to accomplish.

Cursor

The cursor is the flashing line on the screen. The cursor indicates where the text you type will appear.

FILE ORGANIZATION

Like folders in a filing cabinet, MS-DOS uses directories to organize the data stored on a computer.

The root directory (C:\) is the main directory. All other directories are located within this directory.

A path describes the location of a file.

■ The path for this file is c:\letters\personal\john.let

FILE NAME

When you store a file on a computer, you must give the file a name. An MS-DOS file name cannot contain any spaces. A file name consists of a name and an extension, separated by a period.

The name describes the contents of a file and can have up to eight characters.

The extension identifies the type of file and consists of three characters.

UTILITIES

Some versions of MS-DOS include special programs, called utilities, to protect files and optimize a computer. For example, one program finds and repairs disk errors.

Windows 3.1 works with MS-DOS to control the overall activity of a computer. Windows 3.1 is not a true operating system since it needs MS-DOS to operate.

Windows 3.1 displays pictures on the screen to help you perform tasks.

Program Manager

The Program Manager is the control center where you start programs. The Program Manager appears on the screen each time you start Windows 3.1.

Program Icon

A program icon lets you start a program, such as a word processor. An icon is a small picture that represents an object, such as a program.

Window

A window is a rectangle that displays information on the screen. Each window has a title bar that displays the name of the window (example: Accessories).

Group Icon

A group icon contains program icons. For example, the Games group icon contains several games.

Desktop

The desktop is the background area of the screen.

WINDOWS 3.1 FEATURES

Control Panel

The Control Panel lets you change the way Windows 3.1 looks and acts. For example, you can change the colors displayed on the screen.

Accessories

Windows 3.1 provides several accessories, or mini-programs, that let you accomplish simple tasks, such as writing letters and drawing pictures.

File Manager

The File Manager lets you view and organize all the files stored on a computer. Windows 3.1 uses directories to organize information, just as you would use folders to organize papers in a filing cabinet.

WINDOWS FOR WORKGROUPS 3.11

Windows for Workgroups (WfWG) 3.11 is a more powerful version of Windows 3.1. Like Windows 3.1, this program is not a true operating system since it needs MS-DOS to operate.

Windows for Workgroups 3.11 lets you share files and printers with other computers connected to a network and includes programs for electronic mail and scheduling.

Windows 95 is the successor to Windows 3.1. This operating system is more graphical and easier to use than Windows 3.1.

Windows 95 is a true operating system because it does not need MS-DOS to operate.

Window

A window is a rectangle that displays information on the screen. Each window has a title bar that displays the name of the window (example: My Computer).

My Computer

My Computer lets you browse through all the folders and documents stored on a computer.

Recycle Bin

The Recycle Bin stores all the documents you delete and allows you to recover them later.

Network Neighborhood

Network Neighborhood lets you view all the folders and files available on your network.

Start Button

The Start button lets you quickly access programs and documents.

Taskbar

The taskbar contains the Start button and displays the name of each open window on the screen.

Shortcut

A shortcut provides a quick way to open a document or program you use regularly.

WINDOWS 95 FEATURES

Customize Windows 95

You can easily change the way Windows 95 looks and acts. You can change the colors displayed on the screen or adjust the date and time set in the computer.

Document Names

You can use up to 255 characters, including spaces, to name a document in Windows 95. This lets you give your documents descriptive names so they are easy to identify.

Plug and Play

Windows 95 supports Plug and Play technology. This technology lets you add new features to a computer without complex and time-consuming installation procedures.

Windows Explorer

Like a map, Windows Explorer shows you the location of each folder and document on a computer. You can use Windows Explorer to move, open, print or delete documents.

WINDOWS 95 FEATURES (CONTINUED)

WordPad and Paint

Windows 95 comes with a word processing program, called WordPad, that lets you create simple documents such as letters and memos. Windows 95 also includes a drawing program, called Paint, that lets you create pictures.

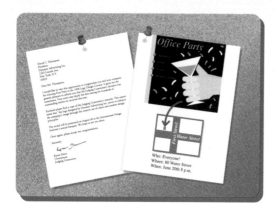

Computer Performance

Windows 95 comes with several features that will improve the performance of a computer. For example, the ScanDisk feature finds and repairs hard disk errors.

Backup

The Backup feature lets you copy important information stored on a computer to floppy disks or tape cartridges. This helps protect the information in case the original files are stolen or damaged due to viruses or computer failure.

Briefcase

The Briefcase feature lets you easily transfer files between your office and portable computers. This feature is useful if you work at home or while traveling. When you return to the office, Briefcase will update any documents you changed.

EXCHANGE INFORMATION

Microsoft Exchange

Windows 95 comes with Microsoft Exchange. This feature lets you exchange electronic mail with other people on a network or the Internet. You can also use this feature to send faxes to other computers or fax machines.

Networking

Windows 95 comes with features that let you share information and printers on a network. The Network Neighborhood feature lets you browse through and access information on all computers on a network. When at home or traveling, you can use the Dial-Up Networking feature to access information on the network at work.

OSR2

OSR2 is the most recent version of Windows 95 and contains many enhancements to the original version. Some of the new components available in OSR2 include Internet applications and a program that allows you to work with scanned documents. Although you cannot purchase the entire OSR2 operating system, you can get individual OSR2 components on the Internet.

Windows 98 is the successor to Windows 95. This operating system is very similar to Windows 95 but includes many new and improved features.

If you have used Windows 95, you will already be familiar with the way Windows 98 looks and works.

My Documents

My Documents provides a convenient place to store your documents.

Internet Explorer

Internet Explorer lets you browse through information on the World Wide Web.

Quick Launch Toolbar

The Quick Launch Toolbar lets you quickly access commonly used features, including Internet Explorer, Outlook Express, the desktop and special Web sites, called channels.

Window

A window often displays a description of the selected item in the window. Most windows also display a toolbar containing buttons you can use to work with items in the window.

Channel Bar

The Channel Bar provides access to special Web sites, called channels, that Windows can automatically deliver to your computer.

WINDOWS 98 FEATURES

Computer Maintenance

Windows 98 is more reliable than Windows 95 and includes many tools you can use to find and fix problems with your computer.

For example, you can use the Maintenance Wizard to perform maintenance tasks on a regular basis, such as checking your hard disk for errors, removing unnecessary files and defragmenting your hard disk to improve its performance.

Computer Optimization

Windows 98 includes many improved features to help you optimize your computer's performance.

For example, the advanced compression utilities in Windows 98 will help you increase the amount of information your hard drive can store.

FAT32

FAT32 is a file system that better manages data on large hard drives to reduce wasted space. Windows 98 can convert your hard drive to FAT32 without disrupting your current programs and documents.

WINDOWS 98 FEATURES (CONTINUED)

Customize Windows 98

Windows 98 offers a large selection of visual effects and desktop themes you can use to customize the way Windows looks. You can customize the appearance of folders by adding a picture to the folder's background. Windows 98 also allows you to view your desktop as a Web page.

Multiple Monitor Capability

Windows 98 has the ability to display the Windows desktop on multiple monitors. This makes working with several open documents or programs easier.

WebTV

Windows 98 makes your computer more entertaining by including a WebTV program. You can use WebTV to watch your favorite television shows on your computer.

Windows Update

Windows 98 provides the Windows Update feature, which lets you access the Windows Update page on the World Wide Web for the latest software updates, new features and technical support information.

WINDOWS 98 AND THE INTERNET

Internet Explorer

Windows 98 includes Internet Explorer 4.0, which is a program that enables you to browse through the information on the World Wide Web. For more information about Internet Explorer, see page 186.

Outlook Express

Windows 98 includes Outlook Express. This program allows you to exchange electronic mail with people around the world. You can exchange messages with friends, colleagues, family members and clients.

FrontPage Express

FrontPage Express is a program you can use to create and edit your own Web pages. You can place pages you create on the Web so people around the world can view your Web pages.

Channels

Windows 98 enables you to access channels on the Internet. A channel is a specially designed Web site that can automatically deliver information from the Internet to your computer.

Windows NT is the most powerful version of the Windows operating system and provides excellent security features.

Windows NT is available in two main versions.

Windows NT Server

Windows NT Server is found on client/server networks. This version of the operating system is designed to support the heavy processing demands of a network server.

The client computers on a network running Windows NT Server can use a variety of operating systems, such as Windows 95, Windows 98 and Mac OS 8.

Windows NT Workstation

Windows NT Workstation is another version of the Windows NT operating system and is used on both client/server and peer-to-peer networks.

Many powerful applications are designed specifically to run on Windows NT Workstation. Many applications designed for the Windows 95 and 98 operating systems will also perform better on Windows NT Workstation.

WINDOWS NT FEATURES

32-bit Operating System

Both main versions of Windows NT are 32-bit operating systems. 32-bit refers to the amount of data processed at one time by the operating system. 32-bit operating systems effectively use the powerful processing capabilities of CPUs such as the Intel Pentium and Digital Alpha.

Ease of Use

The Windows NT operating system is very easy to use. Windows NT has the same look and feel as the Windows 95 and 98 operating systems.

Like other versions of Windows, Windows NT uses a Graphical User Interface (GUI, pronounced "gooey") to interact with the user. GUIs can make many tasks easier.

Support

There are many books and software applications, as well as technical support, available for people who use the Windows NT operating system.

There are also courses designed to certify people who use and maintain the Windows NT operating system.

UNIX is an older, powerful operating system that can be used to run a single user's computer or an entire network.

UNIX is the oldest computer operating system still in widespread use today.

Versions

Many companies have owned UNIX since its development in the late 1960s. Today, there are several versions of the UNIX operating system available.

Popular UNIX operating systems for personal computers include UnixWare by SCO and Linux, which is available for free on the World Wide Web. Other versions of UNIX that are more popular as network operating systems include HP-UX by Hewlett-Packard and AIX by IBM.

Internet

Many of the first computers used to establish the Internet ran the UNIX operating system. Even today, UNIX is the most widely used operating system for servers on the Internet.

UNIX FEATURES

Power

The UNIX operating system is very powerful. UNIX is harder to install and set up than most other operating systems, but provides greater control over a computer's resources and power.

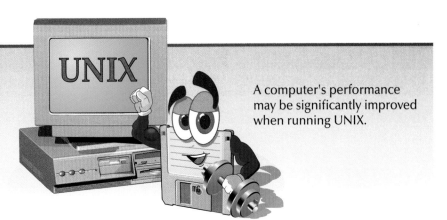

A computer's performance may be significantly improved when running UNIX.

Multitasking

UNIX was originally developed as the operating system for a single large computer, called a mainframe computer. Since multiple users can access a mainframe computer at the same time, UNIX was developed to run many programs and perform numerous tasks at once, called multitasking.

UNIX's multitasking capabilities make it an efficient operating system for networks.

Security

UNIX has many built-in security features to protect information from being accidentally deleted or accessed by unauthorized users.

UNIX's strong security features are one of the reasons UNIX is such a popular operating system on the Internet.

MACINTOSH COMPUTERS

WHAT IS A MACINTOSH?

Macintosh computers, or Macs, were introduced by Apple Computer in 1984. Macs were the first home computers with a mouse, on-screen windows, menus and icons.

MACINTOSH ADVANTAGES

Easy to Use

The graphical interface of a Macintosh makes this type of computer very easy to use.

Desktop Publishing

The fast display of images on screen and true What You See Is What You Get (WYSIWYG) have helped to establish Macintosh computers as the standard in the desktop publishing industry. Desktop publishing lets you create professional documents by integrating text and graphics on a page.

> The most popular types of Macintosh computers are made by Apple Computer.

Power Macintosh

The Apple Power Macintosh is available as a desktop, tower or all-in-one computer. The newest Power Macintosh is called a G3.

A desktop computer usually sits on a desk, under a monitor. A tower computer usually sits on the floor. An all-in-one computer can contain many devices, including a monitor, CD-ROM drive and speakers, in a single unit.

iMac

The iMac is Apple's newest all-in-one computer. This relatively inexpensive computer comes with all the components needed to access the Internet.

PowerBook

The Apple PowerBook is a small, lightweight computer that you can easily transport. Like other notebook computers, PowerBooks have a built-in keyboard and screen. The newest PowerBook is called a G3.

You can buy a PowerBook with the same capabilities as a full-sized computer.

An operating system is the software that controls the overall activity of a computer.

Like the Windows operating systems, Macintosh operating systems use a Graphical User Interface (GUI, pronounced "gooey"). A GUI allows you to use pictures instead of text commands to perform tasks.

System 7

Older Macs use the System 7 operating system. System 7.6 was the final release of System 7.

Mac OS 8

Newer Macs use the more powerful Mac OS 8 operating system. OS 8 has many new features, including an updated desktop, improved Internet capabilities and the ability to work with Windows and MS-DOS files. Mac OS 8.5 will be the next release of OS 8.

PORT

> A port is a connector at the back of a computer where you plug in an external device.

Serial Port

A serial port connects a printer or modem.

Monitor Port

A monitor port connects a monitor.

ADB Port

An Apple Desktop Bus (ADB) port connects a keyboard or mouse.

Audio/Video Port

High-end Macintosh computers have an Audio/Video port that connects a tape deck or VCR. Low-end Macs have only a microphone port and a speaker port.

SCSI Port

A Small Computer System Interface (SCSI) port allows you to attach several separate devices to your computer. SCSI connections are very fast, which makes them ideal for connecting high-speed devices such as external hard drives, removable drives and scanners.

INPUT AND OUTPUT DEVICES

MOUSE

A mouse is a handheld pointing device that lets you select and move items on your screen. Unlike a PC mouse, which has two buttons, a Macintosh mouse has only one button.

KEYBOARD

The keys on a keyboard let you enter information and instructions into a computer. The Macintosh keyboard has a **Command**, or **Apple**, key (⌘ ⌘) that you can use to quickly perform specific tasks. For example, in a word processing document, you can quickly make text bold by pressing the ⌘ ⌘ and B keys.

PRINTER

A printer produces a paper copy of the information displayed on the screen. When buying a printer for a Macintosh, make sure the printer is Mac-compatible. A printer designed for a PC may not work with a Mac.

MONITOR

A monitor displays text and images generated by a computer. Some monitors are designed to work only with Macintosh computers. For more flexibility, you can buy a monitor that will work with both Macs and PCs.

VIDEO CARD

A video card translates instructions from the computer into a form the monitor can understand. Most Macintosh computers come with a built-in video card.

SOUND CHIP

A sound chip allows a computer to play and record high-quality sound. All Macintosh computers come with a built-in sound chip.

MODEM

A modem lets computers exchange information through telephone lines. Most Macintosh modems are external modems. An external modem sits outside a computer and plugs into the back of a computer.

CPU

The Central Processing Unit (CPU), also called a microprocessor, is the main chip in a computer.

A CPU processes instructions, performs calculations and manages the flow of information through a computer system. All new Macintosh computers use Motorola's PowerPC™ microprocessors, also called Reduced Instruction Set Computer (RISC) chips.

The speed of a CPU is measured in megahertz (MHz), or millions of cycles per second.

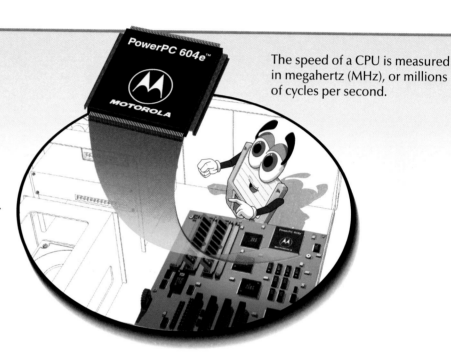

Types of CPUs

603e

The PowerPC™ 603e microprocessor is most often found in older portable Macs and can have speeds of up to 300 MHz.

604e

The PowerPC™ 604e microprocessor is a more powerful CPU found in older desktop Macs and can have speeds of up to 350 MHz.

G3 (750)

The PowerPC™ 750 microprocessor is Motorola's newest CPU and can be found in Apple's new G3 computers. This new CPU can have speeds of up to 300 MHz, but includes more built-in cache, or memory, than earlier generations. This built-in cache further increases the overall speed of the CPU.

BUS

The bus is the electronic pathway in a computer that carries information between devices.

The efficiency of a bus depends on the bus width and the bus speed. Bus speed is measured in megahertz (MHz), or millions of cycles per second.

PCI Bus

The Peripheral Component Interconnect (PCI) bus is found in all new Macintosh computers. The PCI bus can have a width of 32 or 64 bits and speeds of up to 66 MHz.

MEMORY

Memory, also called Random Access Memory (RAM), temporarily stores data inside a computer.

The amount of memory determines the number of programs a computer can run at once and how fast programs will operate.

Capacity

Memory is measured in bytes. You should buy a Macintosh with at least 32 MB of memory, but 64 MB of memory is recommended. You can often improve the performance of a computer by adding more memory.

NETWORKS

INTRODUCTION TO NETWORKS

A network is a group of connected computers that allow people to share information and equipment.

TYPES OF NETWORKS

Local Area Network

A Local Area Network (LAN) is a network that connects computers within a small geographic area, such as a building.

Wide Area Network

A Wide Area Network (WAN) is a network that connects computers across a large geographic area, such as a city or country. A WAN can transmit information by telephone line, microwave or satellite.

NETWORK ADVANTAGES

Work Away From Office

When traveling or at home, you can connect to the network at work to exchange messages and files.

Eliminate Sneakernet

Sneakernet refers to physically carrying information from one computer to another to exchange information. A computer network eliminates the need for sneakernet.

Share Information

Networks let you easily share data and programs. You can exchange documents, electronic mail, video, sound and images.

Share Equipment

Computers connected to a network can share equipment, such as a printer or modem.

NETWORK ADMINISTRATOR

A network administrator manages the network and makes sure the network runs smoothly. A network administrator may also be called a network manager, information systems manager or system administrator.

Network Administrator

Electronic Mail

You can exchange electronic mail (e-mail) with other people on a network. Electronic mail saves paper and provides a fast, convenient way to exchange ideas and request information.

Groupware

Groupware is software that helps people on a network coordinate and manage projects. Groupware packages usually let you exchange electronic mail, schedule meetings, participate in online discussions and share corporate information. Popular groupware packages include Lotus Domino and Novell GroupWise.

Videoconferencing

Videoconferencing allows you to have face-to-face conversations with other people on a network, whether they are around the corner or on the other side of the country.

A computer must have a sound card, speakers and a microphone to transmit and receive sound. The computer must also have a video camera to transmit video images.

Network Traffic

Network traffic is the information that travels through a network. When there is a lot of network traffic, information travels more slowly through the network.

Hub

A hub is a device that provides a central location where all the cables on a network come together.

Network Interface Card

A network interface card is a device that physically connects each computer to a network. This card controls the flow of information between the network and the computer.

Cables

Cables are the wires that connect computers and equipment on a network. There are four main types of cables—coaxial, Unshielded Twisted Pair (UTP), Shielded Twisted Pair (STP) and fiber-optic.

Fiber-optic cable is the most expensive type of cable, but it can carry information faster and over longer distances than other cables.

PEER-TO-PEER NETWORK

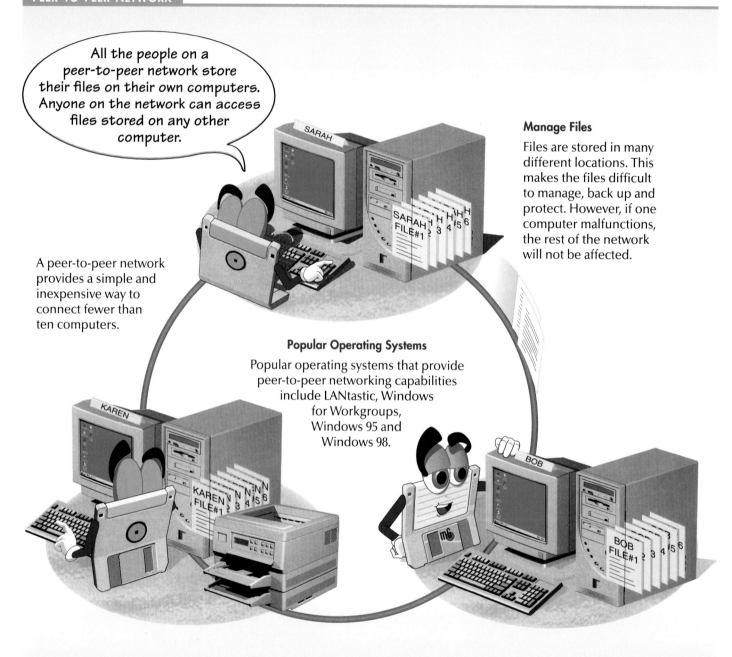

All the people on a peer-to-peer network store their files on their own computers. Anyone on the network can access files stored on any other computer.

Manage Files

Files are stored in many different locations. This makes the files difficult to manage, back up and protect. However, if one computer malfunctions, the rest of the network will not be affected.

A peer-to-peer network provides a simple and inexpensive way to connect fewer than ten computers.

Popular Operating Systems

Popular operating systems that provide peer-to-peer networking capabilities include LANtastic, Windows for Workgroups, Windows 95 and Windows 98.

CLIENT/SERVER NETWORK

> All the people on a client/server network store their files on a central computer. Everyone connected to the network can access the files stored on the central computer.

Server

The server is the central computer that stores the files of every person on the network.

A client/server network provides a highly efficient way to connect ten or more computers, or computers exchanging large amounts of information.

Manage Files

All the files are stored on the server. This makes the files easy to manage, back up and protect. However, if the server malfunctions, the entire network will be affected.

Popular Operating Systems

Popular operating systems that provide client/server networking capabilities include NetWare and Windows NT.

Client

A client is a computer that can access information stored on the server.

ETHERNET

Ethernet is the most popular and least expensive way information can travel through a network. Ethernet is the easiest type of network to set up.

How Ethernet Works

Ethernet works the same way people talk during a polite conversation. Each computer waits for a pause before sending information through a network.

When two computers try to send information at the same time, a collision occurs. After a moment, the computers resend the information.

Speed

Ethernet can transfer information through a network at a speed of 10 megabits per second (Mbps). Fast Ethernet can transfer information through a network at a speed of 100 Mbps. Gigabit Ethernet is a new type of Ethernet that can transfer information through a network at a speed of 1000 Mbps.

TOKEN-RING

Token-ring is a type of network often found in large organizations, such as banks and insurance companies.

How Token-ring Works

Token-ring works by passing a single token from computer to computer. The token collects and delivers information as it travels around the network.

Speed

A token-ring network can send information through a network at speeds of 4 or 16 Mbps.

ATM

Asynchronous Transfer Mode (ATM) is a faster, more powerful way to exchange information on busy networks.

How ATM Works

ATM works by sending information in equal-sized pieces, called cells.

Speed

ATM can send information at speeds of 25, 155 or 622 Mbps.

FIREWALL

A firewall is special software or hardware designed to protect a private computer network from unauthorized access. Firewalls are used by corporations, banks and research facilities to keep information private and secure.

USER NAME AND PASSWORD

You usually have to enter a user name and password when you want to access information on a network. This ensures that only authorized people can use the information stored on the network.

Choose a Password

When choosing a password, do not use words that people can easily associate with you, such as your name or favorite sport. The most effective password connects two words or number sequences with a special character (example: easy@123). To increase security, memorize your password and do not write it down.

Information

An intranet is a very efficient and inexpensive way to make internal company documents available to employees. Companies use intranets to distribute information such as phone directories, product listings and job openings.

Connected Documents

Documents on an intranet are connected. Employees can select highlighted text in one document to display another, related document.

Software

The software used to exchange information on an intranet, such as a Web browser or e-mail program, is the same as the software used to exchange information on the Internet.

THE INTERNET

The Internet is the largest computer network in the world.

In the late 1960s, the U.S. Defense Department began the Internet. The network quickly grew to include scientists and researchers across the country and eventually schools, businesses, libraries and individuals around the world.

The Internet consists of thousands of connected networks around the world. A network is a collection of computers that are connected to share information. Each government, company and organization on the Internet is responsible for maintaining its own network.

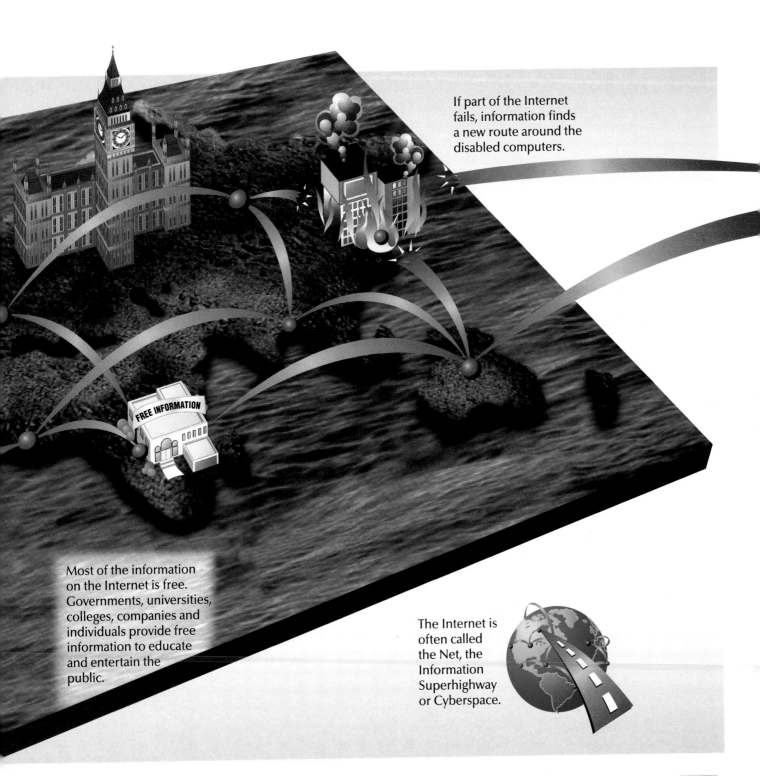

If part of the Internet fails, information finds a new route around the disabled computers.

Most of the information on the Internet is free. Governments, universities, colleges, companies and individuals provide free information to educate and entertain the public.

The Internet is often called the Net, the Information Superhighway or Cyberspace.

ELECTRONIC MAIL

Exchanging electronic mail (e-mail) is the most popular feature on the Internet. You can exchange electronic mail with people around the world, including friends, colleagues, family members, customers and even people you meet on the Internet. Electronic mail is fast, easy, inexpensive and saves paper.

INFORMATION

The Internet gives you access to information on any subject imaginable. You can review newspapers, magazines, academic papers, government documents, television show transcripts, famous speeches, recipes, job listings, works by Shakespeare, airline schedules and much more.

PROGRAMS

Thousands of programs are available on the Internet. These programs include word processors, spreadsheets and games.

ENTERTAINMENT

Hundreds of simple games are available free of charge on the Internet, including backgammon, chess, poker and football.

Using the Internet, you can review current movies, listen to television theme songs, read movie scripts and have interactive conversations with people around the world—even celebrities.

DISCUSSION GROUPS

You can join discussion groups on the Internet to meet people around the world with similar interests. You can ask questions, discuss problems and read interesting stories.

There are thousands of discussion groups on topics such as the environment, food, humor, music, pets, photography, politics, religion, sports and television.

ONLINE SHOPPING

You can order goods and services on the Internet without leaving your desk. You can buy items such as books, computer programs, flowers, music CDs, pizza, stocks and used cars.

All computers on the Internet work together to transfer information around the world.

Packets

When you send information over the Internet, the information is broken down into smaller pieces, called packets. Each packet travels independently over the Internet and may take a different path to arrive at the intended destination.

When information arrives at its destination, the packets are reassembled.

The Future of the Internet

Several organizations are currently developing faster ways of transferring information over the Internet.

Internet2 (I2) will enhance the transfer of information between universities and research facilities in the United States. Project Oxygen, also called the Super-Internet, plans to improve the transfer of complex information, such as video, on the Internet.

TCP/IP

Transmission Control Protocol/Internet Protocol (TCP/IP) is a language computers on the Internet use to communicate with each other. TCP/IP divides information you send into packets and sends the packets over the Internet. When information arrives at the intended destination, TCP/IP ensures that all the packets arrived safely.

Router

A router is a specialized computer that regulates traffic on the Internet and picks the most efficient route for each packet. A packet may pass through many routers before reaching its intended destination.

Backbone

The backbone of the Internet consists of high-speed data lines that connect major networks all over the world.

Download/Upload Information

When you receive information from another computer on the Internet, you are downloading the information.

When you send information to another computer on the Internet, you are uploading the information.

COMPUTER

You can use any type of computer, such as an IBM-compatible or Macintosh computer, to connect to the Internet.

You need specific equipment and programs to connect to the Internet.

PROGRAMS

You need special programs to use the Internet. Most companies that connect you to the Internet provide the programs you need free of charge.

MODEM

You need a modem to connect to the Internet. You should choose at least a 33.6 Kbps modem, although a 56 Kbps modem is recommended. For more information about modems, see page 44.

INTERNET SERVICE PROVIDER

An Internet Service Provider (ISP) is a company that gives you access to the Internet for a fee.

Cost

Many providers offer you a certain number of hours per day or month for a set fee. If you exceed the total number of hours, you are usually charged for every extra hour you use the provider.

Some providers offer unlimited access to the Internet for a set fee. Make sure you are aware of any hidden charges or restrictions.

COMMERCIAL ONLINE SERVICE

A commercial online service is a company that offers a vast amount of information and access to the Internet for a fee.

Popular online services include America Online and The Microsoft Network.

Cost

Most commercial online services let you try their service free of charge for a limited time. After the trial period, most online services offer a certain number of hours per day or month for a set fee. If you exceed the total number of hours, you are usually charged for every extra hour you use the online service.

Some online services offer unlimited access to the service and the Internet for a set fee.

THE WORLD WIDE WEB

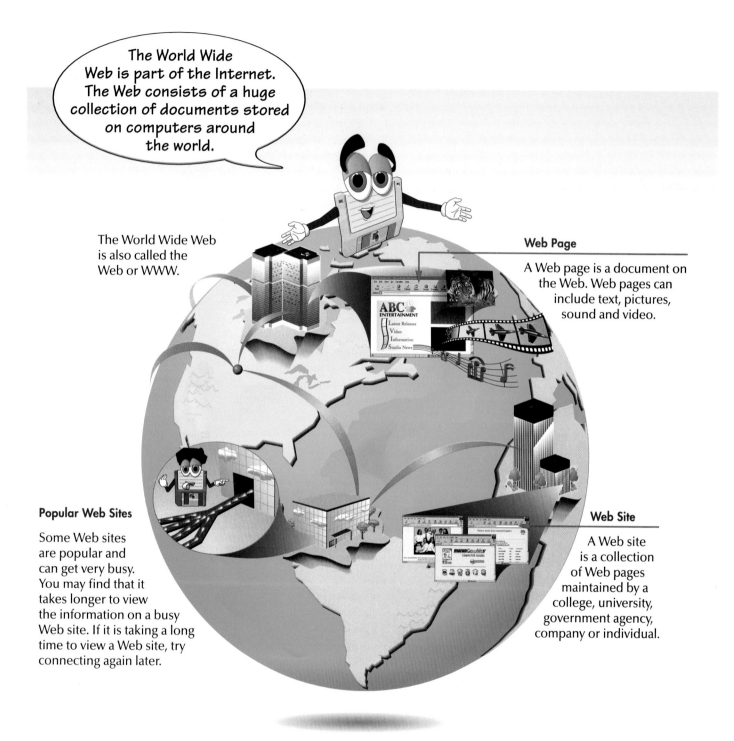

The World Wide Web is part of the Internet. The Web consists of a huge collection of documents stored on computers around the world.

The World Wide Web is also called the Web or WWW.

Web Page

A Web page is a document on the Web. Web pages can include text, pictures, sound and video.

Popular Web Sites

Some Web sites are popular and can get very busy. You may find that it takes longer to view the information on a busy Web site. If it is taking a long time to view a Web site, try connecting again later.

Web Site

A Web site is a collection of Web pages maintained by a college, university, government agency, company or individual.

URL

Each Web page has a unique address, called the Uniform Resource Locator (URL). You can instantly display any Web page if you know its URL.

■ All Web page URLs start with http (HyperText Transfer Protocol).

HYPERTEXT

Web pages are hypertext documents. A hypertext document contains highlighted text that connects to other pages on the Web. You can easily jump from one Web page to another by selecting the highlighted text.

Selecting highlighted text can take you to a page located on the same computer or on a computer across the city, country or world.

A Web browser is a program that lets you view and explore information on the Web.

WEB BROWSER SCREEN

Most Web browsers have a similar look and feel.

■ This area displays the address of the page you are currently viewing.

■ This area displays a Web page.

■ This area displays a toolbar to help you quickly perform common tasks.

HOME PAGE

The home page is the page that appears each time you start your Web browser.

You can choose any page on the Web as your home page. Make sure you choose a home page that provides a good starting point for exploring the Web.

WEB BROWSER FEATURES

Bookmarks

Most Web browsers have a feature called bookmarks or favorites. This feature lets you store the addresses of Web pages you frequently visit. Bookmarks save you from having to remember and constantly retype your favorite Web page addresses.

History List

When you are browsing through pages on the World Wide Web, it can be difficult to keep track of the locations of pages you have visited. Most Web browsers include a history list that allows you to quickly return to any Web page you have recently visited.

Turn Off Graphics

Graphics, or pictures, may take a while to appear on your screen. You can save time by turning off the display of graphics. When you turn off the display of graphics, an icon (example: 🖼️) will appear in place of any graphics.

Graphics On

Graphics Off

INTERNET EXPLORER

Internet Explorer is a popular Web browser from Microsoft.

The latest version of Internet Explorer includes additional programs that you can use to access and exchange information on the Internet.

You can get the latest version of Internet Explorer at the following Web site:

www.microsoft.com

Browse the Web

Internet Explorer integrates the World Wide Web, your corporate network and your Windows 95 or 98 desktop so you can browse through information more efficiently. Internet Explorer also provides enhanced security features so you can safely purchase items on the Internet.

Exchange Electronic Mail

Internet Explorer includes Outlook Express, which enables you to exchange e-mail messages with people around the world. Outlook Express allows you to enhance your messages with graphics, animation and multimedia.

Participate in Newsgroups

You can use Internet Explorer's Outlook Express to join discussion groups, called newsgroups, to meet people around the world with similar interests. There are thousands of newsgroups on many different topics.

Participate in Conferences

Internet Explorer includes NetMeeting, which allows you to easily communicate with another person on the Internet. You can chat with a colleague, exchange files and work together on the same document.

Create Web Pages

Internet Explorer includes FrontPage Express, which allows you to create and edit your own Web pages. You can place pages you create on the Web so people around the world can view your information.

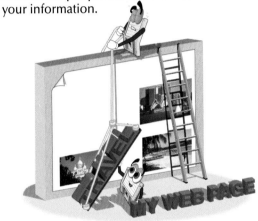

View Channels

Internet Explorer lets you view channels of information. A channel is a Web site that automatically delivers information to your computer at times you specify. Any Web site can be a channel. You can have channels that cover topics such as home decorating, movies, music, news, stocks or travel.

MULTIMEDIA ON THE WEB

Multimedia is an effective way of attracting attention to information on a Web page.

Many companies that advertise on the Web use multimedia–a combination of text, images, sound and video or animation–to sell their products and services.

TEXT AND IMAGES

You can view documents on the Web, such as newspapers, magazines, plays and famous speeches. You can also view images on the Web, such as pictures of celebrities and famous paintings. Most Web pages contain a combination of text and images.

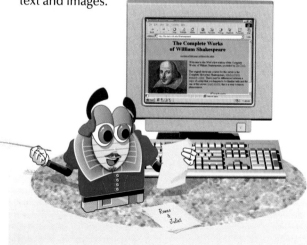

SOUND AND VIDEO

You can listen to sound on the Web, such as TV theme songs, movie soundtracks and historical speeches.

You can also view video on the Web, such as news or movie clips, cartoons and interviews with celebrities.

STREAMING MULTIMEDIA

Streaming multimedia is a system that lets you hear or view continuous sound or video on the Web, such as a live concert or sporting event.

Most Web browsers cannot automatically play streaming multimedia. You must get a program such as RealNetworks RealPlayer or Microsoft NetShow to play streaming multimedia on the Web.

WEB PAGE ENHANCEMENTS

Most new Web browsers can display Java, JavaScript and ActiveX enhancements.

Java

Java is a complex programming language that allows people to create animated and interactive Web pages. Java-enhanced Web pages can display animation and moving text, play music and much more.

JavaScript

JavaScript is a simple programming language that is used mainly for Web page enhancements, such as displaying scrolling messages and fading-in Web pages.

ActiveX

ActiveX is a technology used to improve Web pages. For example, people can use ActiveX to add pop-up menus that instantly display a list of options on a Web page.

A Web portal is a Web site that provides an excellent starting point for exploring the Internet.

Yahoo! is the most popular Web portal. You can visit Yahoo! at www.yahoo.com

Other popular Web portals include:

home.netscape.com

home.microsoft.com

www.excite.com

FIND INFORMATION

All Web portals let you type a word or phrase to quickly search for information of interest on the Web. Web portals also allow you to browse through categories, such as business or sports, to find information that interests you.

FREE SERVICES

Most Web portals offer free e-mail services, which allow you to send and receive e-mail from any computer that has access to the Web.

Web portals also offer free services such as up-to-date news headlines, stock quotes and sports scores, as well as shopping services, maps, and telephone and e-mail directories.

SHOPPING ON THE WEB

You can buy products and services on the Web without leaving your desk.

SHOPPING MALLS

There are shopping malls on the Web where you can view and buy all kinds of products and services.

You can view a list of shopping malls on the Web at:

nsns.com/MouseTracks/HallofMalls.html

Many companies allow you to view and buy their products on the Web.

You can view a list of companies on the Web at:

www.bizweb.com

SECURITY

Security is very important when you want to send confidential information, such as credit card numbers or bank records, over the Internet.

You can safely transfer confidential information to a secure site on the Web. The address of a secure site usually starts with https rather than http.

CHILDREN AND THE WEB

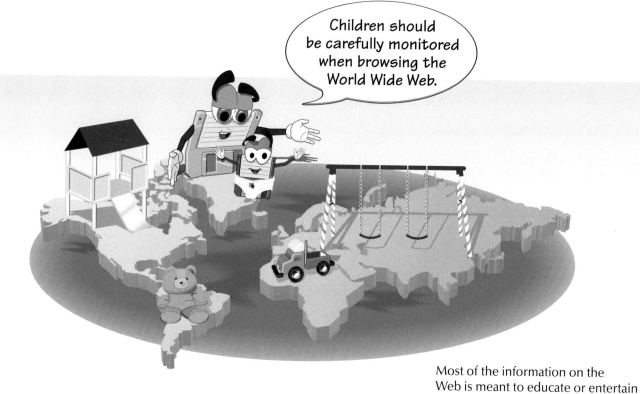

Children should be carefully monitored when browsing the World Wide Web.

Most of the information on the Web is meant to educate or entertain readers, but some sites may contain material you find inappropriate.

TYPES OF INAPPROPRIATE INFORMATION

Pictures

There are many sites on the Web that display pictures meant for adult users. Most adult-oriented sites require verification that users are adults, but the sites often display sample pictures on the first page of the Web site.

Documents

There are many documents on the Web describing everything from causing mischief at school to making explosives. These types of documents may appeal to teenagers and are usually found at Web sites distributing banned or censored books. These Web sites generally do not have any restrictions on who can access the documents.

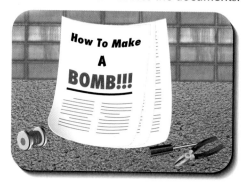

HOW TO RESTRICT ACCESS

Adult Supervision

Constant adult supervision is the best way to ensure that children do not access inappropriate information on the Web.

Before each Web browsing session, the adult and child should decide on the purpose of the session, such as researching a school project. This will help set ground rules for browsing and make the time spent on the Web more productive.

Browser Restrictions

Some Web browsers allow you to restrict the information children can access on the Web. Many Web sites are rated using a system similar to the one used to rate television shows and films.

You can set your Web browser to allow access only to Web sites that comply with specific ratings.

Restriction Programs

You can buy programs that let you restrict access to certain Web sites. Most of these programs provide a frequently updated list of Web sites considered inappropriate for children.

You can purchase restriction programs at the following Web sites:

Cyber Patrol
www.cyberpatrol.com

Net Nanny
www.netnanny.com

CREATE AND PUBLISH WEB PAGES

You can create and publish pages on the World Wide Web to share information with people around the world.

Individuals publish Web pages to share their favorite pictures, hobbies and interests. Companies publish Web pages to promote their businesses, advertise products and publicize job openings.

Organize Ideas

Before you start creating Web pages, decide what ideas you will discuss and how the ideas relate to one another. Break up your information so you discuss only one major idea on each page. You may find it helpful to first sketch the design of your pages on paper.

HTML

HyperText Markup Language (HTML) is a computer code used to create Web pages. There are many programs available, called HTML editors, which can help you create Web pages without learning HTML. Popular HTML editors include Microsoft's FrontPage and Sausage Software's HotDog Pro.

Links

You can add links to your Web pages. A link allows readers to select an image or highlighted text to display another page on the Web. Links are one of the most important features of your Web pages since they let readers move easily through information of interest.

Images

You can add images to your Web pages to make the pages more attractive. You can create these images on your computer, copy them from the Web or use a scanner to copy them from printed material. When copying images that are not your own, be aware of copyright restrictions.

Avoid placing a large number of images on your Web pages. Images increase the time it takes for Web pages to appear on the screen.

Publish Your Web Pages

When you finish creating your Web pages, you can publish the pages by transferring them to a Web server. The company that gives you access to the Internet usually offers space on its Web server where you can publish your Web pages.

ELECTRONIC MAIL AND MAILING LISTS

You can exchange electronic mail (e-mail) with people around the world.

E-mail provides a fast, economical and convenient way to send messages to family, friends and colleagues.

E-MAIL PROGRAM

An e-mail program lets you send, receive and manage your e-mail messages.

Popular e-mail programs include Microsoft Outlook Express and Qualcomm Eudora Pro.

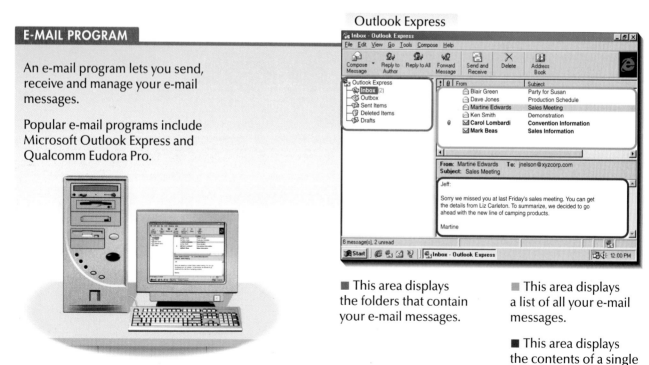

■ This area displays the folders that contain your e-mail messages.

■ This area displays a list of all your e-mail messages.

■ This area displays the contents of a single e-mail message.

E-MAIL ADDRESS

You can send a message to anyone around the world if you know the person's e-mail address.

mvickers@sales.abc.com

mvickers@sales.abc.com

An e-mail address defines the location of an individual's mailbox on the Internet.

PARTS OF AN E-MAIL ADDRESS

An e-mail address consists of two parts separated by the @ ("at") symbol. An e-mail address cannot contain spaces.

mvickers@sales.abc.com

■ The **user name** is the name of the person's account. This can be a real name or a nickname.

■ The domain name is the location of the person's account on the Internet. Periods (.) separate the various parts of the domain name.

ORGANIZATION OR COUNTRY

The last few characters in an e-mail address usually indicate the type of organization or country to which the person belongs.

ORGANIZATION		COUNTRY	
com	commercial	au	Australia
edu	education	ca	Canada
gov	government	ie	Ireland
mil	military	it	Italy
net	network	jp	Japan
org	organization (often non-profit)	uk	United Kingdom

You can send a message to exchange ideas or request information.

mg@maran.com

When you send a message, do not assume the person will read the message right away. Some people may not regularly check their messages.

COST

Once you pay a service provider for a connection to the Internet, there is no charge for sending and receiving e-mail. You do not have to pay extra even if you send a long message or the message travels around the world.

Exchanging e-mail can save you money on long distance calls. The next time you are about to pick up the telephone, consider sending an e-mail message instead.

WRITING STYLE

Make sure every message you send is clear, concise and contains no spelling or grammar errors. Also make sure the message will not be misinterpreted. For example, the reader may not realize a statement is meant to be sarcastic.

MESSAGE TIPS

Smileys

You can use special characters, called smileys or emoticons, to express emotions in messages. These characters resemble human faces if you turn them sideways.

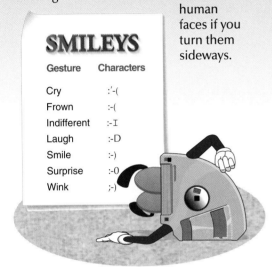

SMILEYS

Gesture	Characters
Cry	:'-(
Frown	:-(
Indifferent	:-I
Laugh	:-D
Smile	:-)
Surprise	:-0
Wink	;-)

Abbreviations

Abbreviations are commonly used in messages to save time typing.

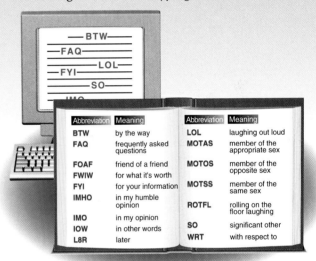

Abbreviation	Meaning	Abbreviation	Meaning
BTW	by the way	LOL	laughing out loud
FAQ	frequently asked questions	MOTAS	member of the appropriate sex
FOAF	friend of a friend	MOTOS	member of the opposite sex
FWIW	for what it's worth		
FYI	for your information	MOTSS	member of the same sex
IMHO	in my humble opinion	ROTFL	rolling on the floor laughing
IMO	in my opinion		
IOW	in other words	SO	significant other
L8R	later	WRT	with respect to

Shouting

A MESSAGE WRITTEN IN CAPITAL LETTERS IS ANNOYING AND HARD TO READ. THIS IS CALLED SHOUTING.

Always use upper and lower case letters when typing messages.

Flame

A flame is an angry or insulting message directed at one person. A flame war is an argument that continues for a while. Avoid starting or participating in flame wars.

RECEIVE A MESSAGE

You do not have to be at your computer to receive a message. Your service provider keeps all your messages until you retrieve them. Make sure you regularly check for messages.

You can use most computers with a modem to connect to your service provider and retrieve messages. This allows you to check your messages while traveling.

REPLY TO A MESSAGE

You can reply to a message to answer a question, express an opinion or supply additional information.

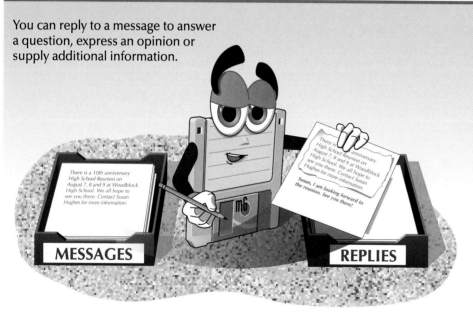

MESSAGES

REPLIES

When you reply to a message, make sure you include part of the original message. This is called quoting. Quoting helps the reader identify which message you are replying to. To save the reader time, make sure you delete all parts of the original message that do not directly relate to your reply.

ATTACH A FILE TO A MESSAGE

You can attach a document, picture, sound, video or program to a message you are sending.

You should keep the size of an attached file under 150 kilobytes. Many computers on the Internet have trouble transferring large attachments.

Many e-mail programs use Multipurpose Internet Mail Extensions (MIME) to attach files to messages.

To view an attached file, the computer receiving the message must be able to understand MIME. The computer must also have a program that can view or play the file.

FORWARD A MESSAGE

After reading a message, you can add comments and then send the message to a friend or colleague.

PRINT A MESSAGE

You can print a message to produce a paper copy of the message.

A mailing list is a discussion group that uses e-mail to communicate.

When a mailing list receives a message, a copy of the message goes to everyone on the mailing list.

There are thousands of mailing lists that cover a wide variety of topics, from aromatherapy to Led Zeppelin. New mailing lists are created every week.

MANUALLY MAINTAINED LISTS

A person manages a manually maintained mailing list.

A manually maintained list usually contains the word "request" in its e-mail address (example: hang-gliding-request@lists.utah.edu).

AUTOMATED LISTS

A computer program manages an automated mailing list. There are three popular programs that manage automated lists—Listproc, Listserv and Majordomo.

An automated list typically contains the name of the program that manages the list in its e-mail address (example: majordomo@teleport.com).

SUBSCRIBE TO A MAILING LIST

Just as you would subscribe to a newspaper or magazine, you can subscribe to a mailing list that interests you.

Subscribing adds your e-mail address to the mailing list.

MAILING LIST
Subscribe Here!
jsmith@xyz.com
kstevens@bookstore.com
bcook@sales.abc.com
dm@maran|

E-mail Addresses
andrew@iog.com
christie@mss.com
julie@bcb.com
noel@cyber.com
tamara@vox.com
ru...23.com

Unsubscribe

If you no longer want to receive messages from a mailing list, you can unsubscribe from the mailing list at any time. Unsubscribing removes your e-mail address from the mailing list.

MAILING LIST ADDRESSES

Each mailing list has two addresses. Make sure you send your messages to the appropriate address.

Mailing List Address

The mailing list address receives messages intended for the entire mailing list. This is the address you use to send messages you want all the people on the list to receive. Do not send subscription or unsubscription requests to the mailing list address.

Mailing List

New Mus Ghost Stories

Administrative Address

The administrative address receives messages dealing with administrative issues. This is the address you use to subscribe to or unsubscribe from a mailing list.

SUBSCRIBE
☐ A Word a Day
wordsmith.org
☐ Bintel
majordomo@world.std.com
☑ Wine
majordomo@niagara.com

Administrative

CHAPTER 13

NEWSGROUPS AND CHAT

INTRODUCTION TO NEWSGROUPS

A newsgroup is a discussion group that allows people with common interests to communicate with each other.

There are thousands of newsgroups on every subject imaginable. Each newsgroup discusses a particular topic such as jobs offered, puzzles or medicine.

Usenet, short for Users' Network, refers to all the computers that distribute newsgroup information.

NEWSGROUP NAMES

The name of a newsgroup describes the type of information discussed in the newsgroup. A newsgroup name consists of two or more words, separated by periods (.).

The first word describes the main topic (example: rec for recreation). Each of the following words narrows the topic.

MESSAGES

A newsgroup can contain hundreds or thousands of messages.

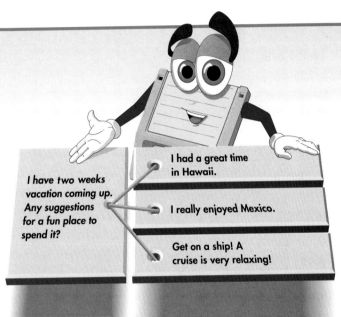

Message

A message is information that an individual posts, or sends, to a newsgroup. A message can be a few lines of text or the length of a book. Messages are also called articles.

I have two weeks vacation coming up. Any suggestions for a fun place to spend it?

I had a great time in Hawaii.

I really enjoyed Mexico.

Get on a ship! A cruise is very relaxing!

Thread

A thread is a message and all replies to the message. A thread may include an initial question and the responses from other readers.

NEWSREADER

A newsreader is a program that lets you read and post messages to newsgroups.

Microsoft Internet Explorer's Outlook Express comes with a built-in newsreader. Other popular newsreaders include MicroPlanet Gravity and Forté Free Agent.

OUTLOOK EXPRESS

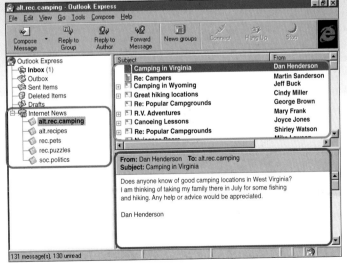

■ This area displays a list of newsgroups.

■ This area displays a list of all the messages in the selected newsgroup.

■ This area displays the contents of a single message.

SUBSCRIBE TO A NEWSGROUP

You can subscribe to a newsgroup you want to read on a regular basis.

If you no longer want to read the messages in a newsgroup, you can unsubscribe from the newsgroup at any time.

READ THE FAQ

A FAQ (Frequently Asked Questions) is a document that contains a list of questions and answers that often appear in a newsgroup.

The FAQ is designed to prevent new readers from asking questions that have already been answered. Make sure you read the FAQ before posting any messages to a newsgroup.

POST A MESSAGE

You can post, or send, a new message to a newsgroup to ask a question or express an opinion. Thousands of people around the world may read a message you post.

alt (alternative)

General interest discussions that can include unusual or bizarre topics.

Examples include:

alt.fan.actors
alt.music.alternative

comp (computers)

Discussions of computer hardware, software and computer science.

Examples include:

comp.security.misc
comp.sys.laptops

news

Discussions about newsgroups in general. Topics range from information about the newsgroup network to advice on how to use it.

Examples include:

news.announce.newgroups
news.newusers.questions

rec (recreation)

Discussions of recreational activities and hobbies.

Examples include:

rec.food.recipes
rec.skydiving

sci (science)

Discussions about science, including research, applied science and the social sciences.

Examples include:

sci.med.dentistry
sci.physics

soc (social)

Discussions of social issues, including world cultures and political topics.

Examples include:

soc.history
soc.women

INTRODUCTION TO CHAT

> You can instantly communicate with people around the world by typing back and forth. This is called chatting.

Chatting is one of the most frequently used features of the Internet.

You can use the chat feature to communicate with family, friends and colleagues in other cities, states or countries without paying long distance telephone charges.

Text-based

Text-based chat is the oldest and most popular type of chat on the Internet. You can have conversations with one or more people. When chatting, the text you type immediately appears on the screen of each person participating in the conversation.

Nicknames

People participating in a conversation often choose nicknames, so you should not assume that people are really who they say they are.

If another person is already using a nickname you want, you must choose a different nickname.

INTERNET RELAY CHAT

Internet Relay Chat (IRC) is a popular chatting system on the Internet. You can join a chat room, or channel, on IRC. Each chat room focuses on a specific topic, such as music or politics.

You need an IRC program to participate in IRC chats. You can get an IRC program at www.mirc.co.uk

INSTANT MESSAGING

Instant messaging lets you chat privately with another person on the Internet.

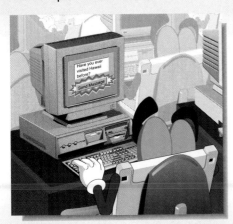

You need a special program to participate in instant messaging. You can get an instant messaging program at www.icq.com

WEB-BASED CHAT

There are sites on the Web that let you chat with other people. All you need to participate in Web-based chat is your Web browser.

You can chat on the Web at www.wbs.net

MULTIMEDIA CHAT

Multimedia chat lets you have voice conversations and communicate through live video over the Internet. You need equipment such as speakers and a video camera to participate in multimedia chat.

You can get Microsoft NetMeeting, a popular multimedia chat program, at www.microsoft.com/netmeeting

INDEX

OVER 6 MILLION

OTHER 3-D Visual SERIES

ORDER FORM

TRADE & INDIVIDUAL ORDERS

Phone: **(800) 762-2974**
or **(317) 596-5200**
(8 a.m.–6 p.m., CST, weekdays)
FAX : **(800) 550-2747**
or **(317) 596-5692**

EDUCATIONAL ORDERS & DISCOUNTS

Phone: **(800) 434-2086**
(8:30 a.m.–5:00 p.m., CST, weekdays)
FAX : **(317) 596-5499**

CORPORATE ORDERS FOR 3-D VISUAL™ SERIES

Phone: **(800) 469-6616**
(8 a.m.–5 p.m., EST, weekdays)
FAX : **(905) 890-9434**

Qty	ISBN	Title	Price	Total

Shipping & Handling Charges

	Description	First book	Each add'l. book	Total
Domestic	Normal	$4.50	$1.50	$
	Two Day Air	$8.50	$2.50	$
	Overnight	$18.00	$3.00	$
International	Surface	$8.00	$8.00	$
	Airmail	$16.00	$16.00	$
	DHL Air	$17.00	$17.00	$

Subtotal _____

CA residents add applicable sales tax _____

IN, MA and MD residents add 5% sales tax _____

IL residents add 6.25% sales tax _____

RI residents add 7% sales tax _____

TX residents add 8.25% sales tax _____

Shipping _____

Total _____

Ship to:

Name_____

Address_____

Company_____

City/State/Zip_____

Daytime Phone_____

Payment: □ Check to IDG Books (US Funds Only)
□ Visa □ Mastercard □ American Express

Card # _____ Exp. _____ Signature_____

maranGraphics™